DevOps for Developers

Michael Hüttermann

Apress®

DevOps for Developers

ISBN-13 (pbk): 978-1-4302-4569-8

ISBN-13 (electronic): 978-1-4302-4570-4

President and Publisher: Paul Manning
Lead Editor: Ben Renow-Clarke
Technical Reviewers: Patrick Debois, Lisa Crispin
Editorial Board: Steve Anglin, Ewan Buckingham, Gary Cornell, Louise Corrigan, Morgan Ertel, Jonathan Gennick, Jonathan Hassell, Robert Hutchinson, Michelle Lowman, James Markham, Matthew Moodie, Jeff Olson, Jeffrey Pepper, Douglas Pundick, Ben Renow-Clarke, Dominic Shakeshaft, Gwenan Spearing, Matt Wade, Tom Welsh
Coordinating Editor: Anamika Panchoo
Copy Editor: Mary Bearden
Compositor: SPi Global
Indexer: SPi Global
Artist: SPi Global
Cover Designer: Anna Ishchenko

Distributed to the book trade worldwide by Springer Science+Business Media New York, 233 Spring Street, 6th Floor, New York, NY 10013. Phone 1-800-SPRINGER, fax (201) 348-4505, e-mail orders-ny@springer-sbm.com, or visit www.springeronline.com.

For information on translations, please e-mail rights@apress.com, or visit www.apress.com.

Apress and friends of ED books may be purchased in bulk for academic, corporate, or promotional use. eBook versions and licenses are also available for most titles. For more information, reference our Special Bulk Sales–eBook Licensing web page at www.apress.com/bulk-sales.

Dedication

For my wife, my two sons, and Doctor Snuggles, my cat.

Contents at a Glance

Contents

About the Author

Michael Hüttermann is a freelance developer and delivery engineer. He offers project support (hands-on as well as conceptual) and gives seminars in the areas of Agile, continuous delivery, and DevOps. An Oracle Java Champion, he has a strong background in software development and considers it essential to experience software in production, not just when it's finished and running on a desktop.

Michael presents at conferences, was the stage producer of the tooling track of Agile 2009, is a driver of the Java user group in Cologne, java.net JUGs community leader, member of Agile Alliance, and member of the JetBrains Academy.

Michael has written three books: *Agile Java Entwicklung in der Praxis* (German, O'Reilly), *Fragile Agile* (German, Hanser, co-author), and *Agile ALM* (Manning).

Michael is based in Cologne, Germany. Further information and contact information can be found at: http://huettermann.net.

About the Technical Reviewers

Patrick Debois has been working on closing the gap between development and operations for many years. In 2009, he organized the first devopsdays.org conference, and thanks to that, the world is now stuck with the term *DevOps*. He is actively involved within the DevOps community by sharing myriad ideas, both technical and cultural, and continuously encourages other people to do the same, especially with employing DevOps ideas within traditional IT enterprises and influencing people toward a collaborative mindset to achieve better results.

Lisa Crispin is the coauthor, with Janet Gregory, of *Agile Testing: A Practical Guide for Testers and Agile Teams* (Addison-Wesley, 2009), coauthor for *Tip House of Extreme Testing* (Addison-Wesley, 2002), and a contributor to *Experiences of Test Automation* by Dorothy Graham and Mark Fewster (Addison-Wesley, 2011) and *Beautiful Testing* (O'Reilly, 2009). She enjoys sharing her experiences through writing, presenting, teaching, and participating in Agile testing communities around the world. Lisa was named one of the 13 "Women of Influence" in testing by *Software Test & Performance Magazine* in 2009. For more about Lisa's work, visit www.lisacrispin.com, @lisacrispin on Twitter, entaggle.com/lisacrispin.

Acknowledgments

First and foremost, I express my very great appreciation to Ben Renow-Clarke, Anamika Panchoo, Kumar Dhaneesh, Louise Corrigan, Mary Bearden, and all others at Apress who helped to bring this project to the shelves.

I wish to acknowledge the help provided by my technical reviewers, Patrick Debois and Lisa Crispin, for their very valuable feedback.

I am particularly grateful for the assistance given by the following contributors:

I thank Aaron Nichols and Lisa Crispin for contributing success stories to Chapter 5.

I thank Heiko Jungholt for contributing to Chapter 7. Heiko calls himself a software addicted IT chameleon with experience as a developer, architect, and project manager who was responsible for IT infrastructure long before the term DevOps was coined.

I thank Tyler Croy and Bastian Spanneberg for their contributions to Chapter 9. Tyler is well known as a strong voice of the Jenkins community who set up and maintains the Jenkins web site. An expert with the tool Puppet, Bastian currently works for the German technology company Codecentric AG, where he does consulting around continuous delivery and DevOps.

I thank John Ferguson Smart for his contribution in Chapter 10. A self-employed consultant, John is well known for his presentations and books on open source tool chains and Agile practices, including acceptance tests.

Introduction

During their daily work of delivering valuable software to customers, too often development and operations are in conflict with each other. Development wants to see their changes (e.g., new features) delivered to the customer quickly, whereas operations is interested in stability, which means not changing the production systems too often.

The gap between development and operations occurs on different levels:

- The incentives gap is a result of different goals of development and operations.

- The process gap results from different approaches of development and operations how to manage changes, bring them to production, and maintain them there.

- The tools gap has its origin from the fact that, traditionally, development and operations often use their own tools to do their work.

As a consequence, development and operations often act like silos, being two distinct teams with suboptimal collaboration.

In organizations, many different settings may be in place that lead to these gaps. Examples include models of management by objectives, a clash of Agile practices and conservative approaches, and a different set of tools, such as Nginx, OpenEJB, and Windows on developers' machines and Apache, JBoss, and Linux on production machines.

DevOps, a portmanteau of development and operations, means to close these gaps by aligning incentives and sharing approaches for processes and tools. DevOps also means to broaden the usage of Agile practices to operations to foster collaboration and streamline the entire software delivery process in a holistic way.

This book helps to bridge the gap between both development and operations. It introduces DevOps as a modern way of bringing development and operations together. Some single aspects of DevOps may not be totally new for you, for example, you may have used the tool Puppet for years already, but the complete set of recipes and the changed mindset toward DevOps form a new way how to serve the customer in the best way possible.

Additionally, by providing real-world use cases (e.g., how to use Kanban or how to release software) and well-grounded background elaborations (e.g., about the danger of moral hazard in projects), this book serves as a reality check for DevOps.

There are many reasons this book can be valuable for you. I hope you'll find some helpful information in it. I wish you much fun and a lot of further success during your projects!

Audience

DevOps for Developers is for software engineers, particularly developers. According to my definition, developers (i.e., people who develop the software) of course includes programmers, but also testers, QA, and system administrators. This book is a perfect choice for engineers who want to go the next step by integrating their approaches for development and delivery of software. This book is also helpful for engineers who want to shape their processes and decide on or integrate open source tools and seek guidance as to how to integrate standard tools in advanced real-world use cases.

What You Will Learn

By reading this book, you will learn:

- What DevOps is and how it can result in better and faster delivered software.

- How to apply patterns to improve collaboration between development and operations.

- How to unify processes and incentives to support shared goals.

- How to start with or extend a tool infrastructure that spans project roles and phases.

- How to address pain points in your individual environment with appropriate recipes.

- How to break down existing walls that create an unnecessarily sluggish delivery process.

Book Structure

This book is divided into four parts:

- *Part I Fundamentals:* This part provides the fundamentals of DevOps, including the definition of DevOps. We'll discuss the building blocks of DevOps. Part I contains the basics, which provide an understanding that is the basis for the following parts.

- *Part II Metrics and Measurement View:* This part digs deeper into approaches to share and align goals and incentives. You'll learn that quality and testing are crucial aspects of DevOps as well as team work.

- *Part III Process View:* This part is dedicated to the DevOps aspects that are relevant to processes. We'll discuss practices for achieving a holistic approach to bridging development and operations.

- *Part IV Technical View:* This final part will examine the technical components that comprise DevOps. You'll learn basics and tools for automating the release process to gain faster feedback. Other major aspects included here are infrastructure such as code and specification by example.

The areas of individual sections may overlap slightly, but they generally have a dedicated, strong focus on the important concepts of DevOps. The order of parts shows that the most important facets of DevOps are people, incentives, and goals, followed by processes and then technical fractions. The chosen breakdown of this book allows you to navigate to different parts and chapters as well as read the book from start to end.

Fundamentals

This part provides the fundamentals of DevOps, including the definition of DevOps, its building blocks, and how it can benefit your work.

Beginning DevOps for Developers

Confuse of Dev or Ops? Simple rule: if you are praise for Web site success, you are Dev; if you are blame when Web site down, you are Ops.

—DevOps Borat[1]

Welcome to *DevOps for Developers*. This book discusses approaches, processes, and tools for optimizing collaboration between software development and operations and bringing Agile approaches to all parts of the streamlined software delivery process.

This chapter provides all the necessary information to help you understand what DevOps is and how you can proceed in this area based on this understanding. This chapter will explain the natural conflicts that exist between development and operations and where DevOps can help address those conflicts. It will explain the history and movements that have influenced DevOps as well as the perspectives and activities that comprise DevOps. In addition to exploring the core concepts underlying DevOps, we will also explore what DevOps is *not*.

For now, however, we will begin by presenting the definition of DevOps.

The Definition of DevOps

Isolated aspects of DevOps have been well known for years, whereas others are new. However, no unified term exists that encompasses all of the aspects of DevOps. The term *DevOps* is widely used these days, and many different types of content are associated with it.

---

[1] http://twitter.com/devops_borat/status/52857016670105600.

As you read these chapters, keep in mind that many different definitions of DevOps exist and that this book delivers one specific definition, which approaches DevOps from the developer perspective. This book will show that DevOps is really a mix of well-known, advanced practices and new, innovative approaches to common challenges in project life software delivery and operations.

■ **Note** This book primarily targets developers. Be aware of the fact that the term *developers* does not only refer to testers, programmers, and quality assurance experts. Rather, the "one team approach" (which I'll introduce in this book) also includes experts from operations who develop, for instance, scripts or "infrastructure as code."

The term DevOps is a blend of development (representing software developers, including programmers, testers, and quality assurance personnel) and operations (representing the experts who put software into production and manage the production infrastructure, including system administrators, database administrators, and network technicians). DevOps describes practices that streamline the software delivery process, emphasizing the learning by streaming feedback from production to development and improving the cycle time (i.e., the time from inception to delivery; see more about this process in Chapter 3). DevOps will not only empower you to deliver software more quickly, but it will also help you to produce higher-quality software that is more aligned with individual requirements and basic conditions.

DevOps encompasses numerous activities and aspects, such as the following[2]:

- *Culture*: People over processes and tools. Software is made by and for people.

- *Automation*: Automation is essential for DevOps to gain quick feedback.

- *Measurement*: DevOps finds a specific path to measurement. Quality and shared (or at least aligned) incentives are critical.

- *Sharing*: Creates a culture where people share ideas, processes, and tools.

WHAT DOES THE TERM DEVOPS MEAN?

The term DevOps is a blend of development and operations.

The term DevOps did not come about overnight. Instead, many movements and people have influenced the development of DevOps, which we'll explore next.

---

[2] Also known as CAMS. See John Willis, http://www.opscode.com/blog/2010/07/16/what-devops-means-to-me.

Influences and Origins

Patrick Debois coined the term DevOps in 2009 while organizing the DevOpsDays conference in Belgium.[3] This was the first in a series of relevant conferences dedicated to the concept that helped spread the popularity of the term. Many past movements, early adopters, and influences helped coin DevOps and transform DevOps into an accepted term:

- *Patrick Debois* ran a session called "Agile Operations and Infrastructure: How Infra-gile Are You?"[4] at the Agile 2008 conference in Toronto and published a paper with a similar name.[5]

- *Marcel Wegermann* published a e-mail list called "Agile System Administration."[6]

- *John Allspaw* gave a presentation called "10+ Deploys per Day: Dev and Ops Cooperation"[7] at the Velocity 2009 conference in San Jose.

- *Steven Blank* published a book called *Four Steps to the Epiphany*.[8]

- *Eric Ries* published *The Lean Startup*[9] and others have written on the "lean startup" scene.

- *The 451 Group* published the first analyst report on DevOps (titled "The Rise of DevOps"[10]) in September 2010.

Labeling tools or approaches as being aligned with "DevOps" without reflecting on the concrete content or without trying to define DevOps tends to result in random buzzwords. Thus, one may ask what is the motivation for the DevOps movement? To understand this motivation better, we'll now examine the underlying conflict between development and operations.

Development and Operations in Conflict

Traditional organizations divide their teams by type of work (that often results in what are called silos). Certain development departments specialize in writing code. Many companies also have dedicated departments for testing software. Because bringing software to production and maintaining it there often require skills other than software development, an operations department is created. Splitting work areas appears to benefit the management as well. In addition to the specialized team, each department has its own manager who fulfills the individual requirements needed for this specific department.

---

[3] http://www.devopsdays.org/events/2009-ghent/.
[4] http://submissions2008.agilealliance.org/node/424/.
[5] http://www.jedi.be/presentations/IEEE-Agile-Infrastructure.pdf.
[6] groups.google.com/group/agile-system-administration.
[7] http://www.slideshare.net/jallspaw/10-deploys-per-day-dev-and-ops-cooperation-at-flickr.
[8] Cafepress.com, 2005.
[9] Crown Business, 2011.
[10] https://www.451research.com/report-long?icid=1304.

Each department defines its goals based on the division of labor. The development department may be measured by its speed in creating new features, whereas the operations department may be judged by server uptime and application response time. Unfortunately, operations is considered to be successful if the metrics are stable and unchanging, whereas development is only applauded if many things change. Because conflict is baked into this system, intensive collaboration is unlikely.

Development teams strive for change, whereas operations teams strive for stability (the definitions of change and stability will be discussed in Chapter 2). The conflict between development and operations is caused by a combination of conflicting motivations, processes, and tooling. As a result, isolated silos evolve (see Figure 1-1).

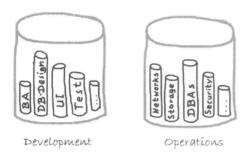

Figure 1-1. *Development and operations are two distinct departments. Often, these departments act like silos because they are independent of each other* [11]

In a nutshell, the conflict between development and operations is as follows:

- *Need for change*: Development produces changes (e.g., new features, bug fixes, and work based on change requests). They want their changes rolled out to production.

- *Fear of change*: Once the software is delivered, the operations department wants to avoid making changes to the software to ensure stable conditions for the production systems.

However, there is a long history of software engineering and process improvements. What about the "Agile" approach? Does the Agile method address those pain points?

Both development and operations groups will optimize themselves. Instead of optimizing the whole process, development and operations teams improve their individual processes to meet their respective objectives. Developers primarily focus on accelerating the creation of new features by, for instance, adopting Agile methodologies. The Agile movement has brought together programmers, testers, and business representatives. Conversely, operations teams are isolated groups that maintain stability and enhance performance by applying practices such as the Information Technology Infrastructure Library (ITIL),[12] which equates change to risk.

The more specialized the individual departments are, the worse the results for the company and its projects. The development department continually creates new features, changes, or bug fixes and throws them over the wall to operations. The operations department, in turn, perfects its many defense mechanisms to prevent change.

---

[11] My thanks to Udo Pracht for the idea of this figure.

[12] http://www.itil-officialsite.com.

The conflict between the two groups can only be healed and the silos bridged by aligning the two groups' different goals. To do so, Agile methods must be applied to operations as well. We'll explore this concept in the next section.

Broaden the Usage of Agile

Projects often go through the following phases:

- *Inception*: In this interval, the vision of the system is developed, a project scope is defined, and the business case is justified.

- *Elaboration*: In this interval, requirements are gathered and defined, risk factors are identified, and a system architecture is initialized.

- *Construction*: In this interval, the software is constructed, programmed, and tested.

- *Transition*: In this interval, the software is delivered to the user.

- *Operations*: In this interval, the software is available to the user and is maintained by the operations team.

▨ **Note** These intervals apply to all types of process models, including traditional, phased, and modern ones, based on either increments (small unit of functionality) or iterations (mini-projects that may result in an increment).

Agile software development has helped to bring together different project roles, including programmers, testers, and quality assurance (QA) personnel. These different experts comprise the cross-functional development team. This "one team approach" brought them together more closely than they had been before the Agile movement hit the market. Agile software development is now mainstream. The principles of Agile methods are focused on defining, building, and constructing software (see Figure 1-2).

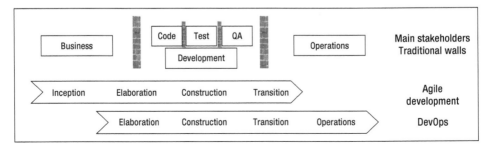

Figure 1-2. *Agile software development spans the process from inception to transition. DevOps spans the process from elaboration to operations, and often includes departments such as HR and finance*

■ **Note**   It can make sense to broaden DevOps to departments like finance and human resources (HR) because of the influence DevOps has on those departments. For example, new colleagues (who are hired by HR) will need to have the soft skills (like communication skills) to work according to the DevOps approach. Another example is the finance department, or the comptroller, that has to transform and collect its metrics and measurements toward DevOps.

Agile efforts often end at the transition phase from development to operations. The delivery of software (i.e., lean practices for shipping the software to production and making it available to the end users) is covered by DevOps. DevOps provides patterns to foster collaboration among project stakeholders and uses processes as well as tools to streamline the software delivery process and reduce the overall cycle time.

Next, we examine the possible views of DevOps.

Views of DevOps

The fundamental bases for successful DevOps are a culture of trust and a feeling of fellowship. Everything starts with how people perceive one another. That is, does the company have an "us vs. them" culture or a "we" culture? Thus, DevOps centers on the concept of "sharing": sharing ideas, issues, processes, tools, and goals.

WHAT IS DEVOPS?

DevOps is a mix of patterns intended to improve collaboration between development and operations. DevOps addresses shared goals and incentives as well as shared processes and tools. Because of the natural conflicts among different groups, shared goals and incentives may not always be achievable. However, they should at least be aligned with one another.

DevOps respects the fact that companies and projects have specific cultures and that people are more important than processes, which, in turn, are more important than tools. DevOps accepts the inevitability of conflicts between development and operations.

The DevOps movement aims to improve communication between developers and operations teams to solve critical issues, such as fear of change and risky deployments. Ideally, the DevOps principles need support from tools to be fully realized and provide the automation required. Tools in each part of the workflow have evolved in their own silos and with the support of their own target teams. A DevOps mentality requires a seamless, highly integrated process from the start of development to the end of production deployments and maintenance. To help automate and integrate all of the essential delivery steps in a holistic way, the DevOps approach also needs lightweight tool changes. Collaboration between development and operations starts well before the deployment of software and continues long afterward.

With DevOps, all stakeholders of the delivery process work together closely and share the same goals. No isolated silos exist in the software delivery process. Rather, stakeholders collaborate closely. DevOps can be examined from the following overlapping perspectives:

- *Metrics and measurement view*: This aspect addresses quality and testing and stresses shared incentives.

- *Process view*: This aspect covers congruence and flow to gain fast feedback and set up a holistic process.

- *Technical view*: This aspect discusses fast feedback through automation, particularly automatic releasing, specification by example, and infrastructure as code.

If you think that this list covers a wide area of topics that need to be discussed in much more detail, you'd be absolutely correct. The chapters of this book are aligned with these perspectives, and we'll explore each of them in detail.

After discussing the definition of DevOps, we'll now explain what DevOps is not.

What DevOps Is NOT

The term DevOps is a slightly overloaded one. To understand the scope of the DevOps concept, it helps to discuss what DevOps is not. DevOps is not a marketing (buzz) term. Although some aspects of DevOps are not new, it is a new and strong movement intended to improve the delivery process. The DevOps approach accepts the daily challenges in software delivery and provides steps to address them. DevOps does not allow developers to work on the production system. It is not a free "process" that opens production-relevant aspects to developers. For example, DevOps does not grant developers permission to work on production systems. Instead, DevOps is about discipline, conventions, and a defined process that is transparent for all.

Roles and Structures

DevOps is not a new department (see Figure 1-3). Every attempt to establish a DevOps-type department leads to bizarre constructions. Some people believe that "NoOps"[13] is the future,

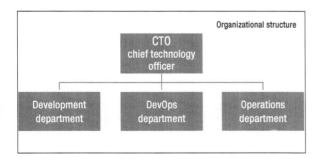

Figure 1-3. *DevOps is not a new department. If you see an organizational structure that shows a DevOps item, please point the decision makers to this book*

---

[13] See http://blogs.forrester.com/mike_gualtieri/11.02-07-i_dont_want_devops_i_want_noops.

where developers are in charge of all relevant aspects of software production. Of course, such a scenario is impossible; developers and operations engineers have different priorities and skills. Similarly, the opposite is not true: DevOps does not mean that operations' experts take over all development tasks.

"Responsibilities can, and do, shift over time, and as they shift, so do job descriptions. But no matter how you slice it, the same jobs need to be done, and one of those jobs is operations"[14] and the other is development. Thus, DevOps is also not a new role profile that will supplant current developers and operations experts. DevOps describes patterns for collaboration, processes, and tools; it is not a new job title (see Figure 1-4). As soon as you understand the DevOps concept, you'll see how strange the very idea of hiring a "DevOp" is.

Experienced DevOps engineer required

We want you!

This position offers:
Shuttle service between departments
Fame and honor
Opportunity to advance to Principal DevOps Engineer
Work/Life balance on Sundays

Applicants should have:
Verbal/Nonverbal communication skills
Excellent knowledge of DevOps tool suites
At least average anti-silo thinking
General understanding of chaos theory

 Apply now!!
Contact Information
(999) 11 22 33 44

Figure 1-4. *DevOps is not a new job. If you see a job advertisement that asks for a DevOps expert, please point the author of the ad to this book*

Some people may make the following claim: "DevOps is a catalog of recipes: implement them all, and you are done." This statement is false because you will focus on finding the best solution for your individual situation by implementing DevOps. There is no one-size-fits-all solution, and no "DevOps-by-the-book" approach will solve all of your problems.

---

[14] See http://radar.oreilly.com/2012/06/what-is-devops.html

Others will claim that "DevOps will lose importance as Cloud solutions gain popularity; platform as a service (PaaS) solutions will make DevOps unnecessary." This objection is an interesting one, but the truth is that Cloud solutions introduce another abstraction level and do not supplant operations. There is no need for the Cloud to do DevOps.

Aligning existing structures and roles with DevOps is a process. Many books exist that focus on strategies to come up with working agreements across teams[15] or to how introduce new ideas and change.[16]

DevOps and Tool Suites

Some people prefer to think about tools instead of people and processes. Without respecting other people and understanding processes, these people merely introduce tools. What happens if there are issues with using tools in a project? Some people may recommend that you "just introduce new tools." With DevOps, the same problem emerges. Without understanding the idea behind the approach, attempting to improve collaboration, and sharing processes in a concrete way, every attempt to adopt DevOps methods will fail. Labeling individual tools as DevOps tools is acceptable, but please don't think of DevOps as a new tool for eliminating operations staff or as a tool suite (see Figure 1-5); rather it's an approach for freeing up time of the current staff to focus on harder problems that can deliver even more business value.

Figure 1-5. *DevOps is not a tool suite. If you see a tool suite labeled as a "DevOps" suite, ask the vendor to read this book*[17]

DevOps may bring together subprocesses to form a comprehensive delivery process that enables software to be delivered at high speed and at a high quality. However, DevOps does not necessarily introduce new tools. A specific new tool can be used to implement a given process.

---

[15] See Diana Larsen and Ainsley Nies, *Liftoff, Launching Agile Teams & Projects* (Onyx Neon, 2012).
[16] See Mary Lynn Manns and Linda Rising, *Fearless Change, Patterns for Introducing new Ideas* (Addison-Wesley, 2005).
[17] My thanks to Udo Pracht for the idea of this figure.

However, in most cases involving DevOps, preexisting tools are orchestrated and integrated for use by development and operations teams. For example, a version control system may be used not only to store code and build scripts and tests but also to create infrastructure behavior. The time for silo solutions, where tools are only used for a specific project role, is over!

▧ **Note**   Tool vendors can be expected to label their tools as DevOps tools. Take such labels with a grain of salt. Tools can be shared between development and operations teams and can be named "DevOps tools." However, people and processes are more important than tools.

Structure of This Book

This book is split into the following four parts:

- *Part I Fundamentals*: This chapter is included in this part, which provides information about the fundamentals of DevOps. Here we discuss the definition of DevOps and elaborate the path from traditional software engineering to DevOps. We'll discuss the building blocks of DevOps. Part I contains the basics, which provide an understanding of and the basics for the following parts.

- *Part II Metrics and Measurement View*: This part digs deeper into approaches to share and align goals and incentives. You'll learn that quality and testing are crucial aspects of DevOps.

- *Part III Process View*: This part is dedicated to the DevOps aspects that are relevant to processes. We'll discuss practices for achieving a holistic approach to bridging development and operations.

- *Part IV Technical View*: This final part will examine the technical components that comprise DevOps. You'll learn basics and tools for automating the release process to gain fast feedback. Other major aspects included here are infrastructure such as code and specification by example.

The areas of individual sections may overlap slightly, but they generally have a dedicated, strong focus on the important portions of DevOps. The order of parts shows that the most important facets of DevOps are people, incentives, and goals, followed by processes and then technical fractions. The chosen breakdown of this book allows you to navigate to different parts and chapters as well as read the book from start to end.

Conclusion

DevOps is a movement that addresses the natural conflict between software development and operations. The conflict results from divergent goals and incentives. DevOps improves collaboration between development and operations departments and streamlines the complete delivery process in a holistic way. Three perspectives (a metrics and measurement view, a process view, and a technical view) will help us examine the ingredients of DevOps.

In the remaining chapters of this first part, we'll continue to shape the definition of DevOps. In Chapter 2, I'll explain in further detail what DevOps is. We'll discuss the long journey from dedicated coding, testing, QA, and operations teams to a holistic approach that spans all types of different people. In Chapter 3, you'll learn about the building blocks of DevOps that are fundamental to the upcoming parts: the metric and measurement view, the process view, and the technical view. Those perspectives will be covered in detail throughout the rest of this book.

After setting the stage and discussing the core concepts of DevOps, we are now ready to proceed to Chapter 2, which will explain the movement from traditional software engineering to DevOps.

Introducing DevOps

In Agile is all about fail quick. If you have success in company you do Agile wrong.

—DevOps Borat[1]

In this chapter, I'll introduce the concept of DevOps. I'll also summarize in which areas traditional projects suffer, what Agile has done in the past several years to improve this situation, and what is nevertheless still missing in many projects today. With Agile, testers and programmers became developers, and with DevOps, developers and operations become DevOps. I will show that natural conflicts between developers and operations often lead to the "blame game," which can be resolved through use of the DevOps approach. DevOps leads to a "one team" approach where programmers, testers, and system administrators are involved in the development of the solution.

We will begin our journey toward DevOps with a brief description of the traditional approaches in software engineering and their major attributes.

Traditional Project Settings

Software applications consist of functionality, and in many cases, new functionality will often be continuously introduced. Only features that ship with the product add value and form and improve upon a "solution." A solution is more than a set of features; a solution is an application that adds value and benefits the user (the person using the application) and the customer (the person with the money).

Newly developed features only add value if these new features are available not only in a developer's workspace or in a test machine but also in the production environment. The production environment comprises the hardware configuration of servers, the central processing

---

[1] http://twitter.com/devops_borat/status/116916346222157824.

units (CPUs), the amount of memory, the spindles, the networking infrastructure that connects the environments, the configuration of operating systems, and the middleware (e.g., the messaging system applications as well as the web servers and database servers that support the application).

For the software, it's a long journey to its destination: the production system. In traditional project settings, software is usually specified and then programmed in stages rather than in iterations or increments. During programming, specifications often prove to be insufficient, wrong, or inconsistent. The customer files a batch of change requests that must be tracked and brought together with the original specs and their implementation.

Testers and QA do their best to detect bugs in their down-streamed activities, which starts when software is created. Testers are often blamed for all software bugs that show up.

Ticket systems fill up with entries. Some may even find a large number of tickets helpful because they prove that good tests have found many bugs or can serve as a parking lot for new features. Few operators recognize numerous tickets as a waste because maintaining ticket systems may already be an expensive nightmare, and parked tickets are by no means a replacement for shipped features.

Some decision makers believe that quality can be injected post mortem by adding testers and QA to the project. Metrics assessing the software quality are collected and forwarded to the team. In some cases, people in ivory towers (or worse still, the development team) judge the developed product after the fact with strange audits or academic standards.

In many projects, there is a start point and a defined end, people work in the project, money is restricted, and the to-be-delivered functionality is specified. The term *project* is traditionally defined in this manner. To develop and deliver the software, project leaders define and introduce the project roles, which are specialized according to the different aspects of the overall process. All this is done to organize the work and to improve the results. In many cases, projects are finished successfully. Countless variations of that approach and comparisons of all those approaches (with or without including Agile methodologies) are outside the scope of this book. But what is important to understand here is that, even in successful projects, certain attributes may evolve, including:

- *Hero cult*: The team is nothing, and individuals are king. For example, consider a programmer who fails to document his or her work adequately and delivers low-quality software. The bad software requires new adjustments and bug fixes that can only be performed by the hero creator because he or she did not document or share his or her knowledge, decisions, and project experience with the team.

- *Emphasis on titles*: Everyone in the team plays a role, which has a fancy description. Title is king! One person is only a developer, but another is a senior developer. What is the process behind a person's promotion to a senior, to a principal, or to whatever categories are in place within a company? Often, the primary factor is the duration of the person's membership in the company, and the title does not say anything about the person's technical skills or soft skills, such as his or her ability to cooperate and communicate.

- *Shadow responsibilities*: Although role descriptions list clear responsibilities, people try their best to avoid performing their duties. Alternatively, they pursue other activities that are not part of their responsibilities simply to protect their turf and to ensure their influence or to indulge their "pet projects." As a result, you have a gap (or a misperception) between a described process (with roles and responsibilities) and the way in which the process is lived in the project.

- *Favor a plan over planning*: Everything is planned, but the activity of planning is seldom performed. Planning (i.e., adjusting the original plan) is a rare activity. For example, once a plan exists in the form of a Gantt chart (a chart developed by Henry Gantt to specify the start and finish dates in projects; this chart is used to plan and control work and record progress), the chart becomes the leading medium and the goal of the project. In this case, the goal no longer is to deliver software that adds value to the customer in a quick and efficient manner. This often leads to beautiful but isolated castles.

DEVELOPMENT AND OPERATIONS

In traditional settings, the term *development* describes the programmers in the team. Testers and QA are often dedicated project roles whose activities start after the programmers have finished their work. *Operations* contains database administrators, system administrators, network administrators, and other types of administrators who set up and maintain the server and systems. The operations group essentially accompanies and accounts for the "last mile" in the delivery process. In the classic approach, they are not always involved in the work of programmers, testers, and QA, but they obtain the final result of their work.

The previously listed attributes often result in different organizational and cultural barriers, including the following:

- *Separate teams*: With luck, you'll have separated teams; if you are unlucky, you'll be part of some loosely coupled working groups. In other words, separated teams will foster their positions and pursue individual interests and goals. Unfortunately, a collection of great teams is not a replacement for one team that pursues a unified and shared project goal.

- *No common language*: Specialized teams and project roles prefer to use the language that is most comfortable for them. Instead of using a shared language that the whole project understands or (even better) a language that is also understood by the user and customer, many small, highly specialized terms are used. As a result, misunderstandings occur. Highly specialized languages also tend to be too technical to serve as an accurate vehicle of customer communication.

- *Fear*: What others do is bad, and any activities by other people that could impact one's own type of work or activities are confronted with skepticism. Perceiving shared goals and knowledge as risky will lead to fear on all sides, especially fear of losing power, influence, and reputation. History and habits have their roles as well. People don't want to give up on old habits unless they have good reasons to accept the new way of doing things.

■ **Note**　I once worked in a project where four developers worked on the same software while sitting in one room at one table. Each of these guys referred to their colleagues as their "team," which meant that four teams sat at that table instead of one.

In the worst-case, waterfall-like scenario, programmers code the application that is tested by testers afterward. QA performs down-streamed quality assurance afterward. The walls (in the form of organizational or process borders) between different groups prevent close collaboration. After years of suffering, Agile concepts entered the market and helped to eliminate these barriers.

Agile Project Settings

The Agile movement addressed the pains of suboptimal collaboration and divergent goals. The "one team" approach fosters communication and collaboration by bringing different parties together to form one team that shares the same goals (i.e., successful software development). The term *developer* takes on a different meaning because both programmers and testers develop the software. Programmers and testers work together seamlessly and comprise the working group known as developers.

Many projects experience the best results by allowing one team of programmers and testers to work closely together and conduct the entire QA. Everyone in the team performs QA and is responsible for quality. As Figure 2-1 shows, the one team approach results in team development, whereas the operations end is still essentially isolated from the development of the software.

In Agile project settings, roles, and responsibilities change. Roles are blurred, and each team member wears different hats. Programmers are paid to perform tasks other than writing code, and testers do more than test. Testers also help programmers to create better code.

As a result, we have a changed approach, as shown by the following:

- *Quality*: Testers are not solely responsible for quality; rather, the whole team works together to maintain quality.

- *Development*: Programmers do not code alone; rather, everyone helps them to understand what to code.

- *Project roles*: Cross-functional teams are set up and roles are decoupled from activities.

If you define work as activities to be accomplished together, you break down role boundaries and allow team members to add value in multiple areas. For example, you can enable programmers to conduct exploratory tests. Similarly, you can allow QA leads to work with the application code if they find a fixable bug.

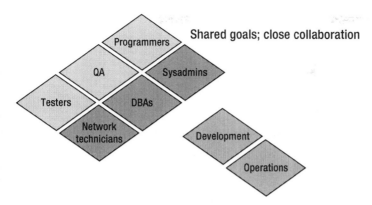

Figure 2-1. *Agile software development brings together programmers, testers, and QA to form the development team. The operations group, with its individual subareas, is still isolated from development*

DEVELOPMENT AND OPERATIONS IN AGILE

In Agile approaches, development consists of programmers, testers, and QA. Operations often acts as a silo (or is treated as a silo, depending on the perspective).

Agile approaches claim to produce happier participants. However, the operations department is still perceived by some as a strange group of highly specialized server techies in the engine room.

In contrast to the developers, the operations team is tasked with taking the deliverables received from the development team and making the software available on production machines such that the software can be used by the users. At the same time, the operations team often receives nonfunctional requirements (such as target values for the availability of the application). The shipped software (delivered by development team) may conflict with these nonfunctional requirements.

Many different activities are important for operations. For example, the operations group is responsible for deploying new software releases and managing the stability and availability of the production systems, including servers, networks, and other environmental facets.

A DEFINITION OF STABILITY

Stability is often defined as a resilient system that keeps processing transactions, even if transient impulses (rapid shocks to the system), persistent stresses (force applied to the system over an extended period), or component failures disrupt normal processing (see Michael Nygard, *Release It!*, The Pragmatic Programmers, 2007, p. 25).

Thus, operations is responsible for the availability of the software in production, and its success is often measured with metrics that calculate server uptimes, software availabilities, security, capacity (including scalability, longevity, throughput and load), and response times. These metrics (see more on the metrics in Chapter 4) are commonly defined as quality requirements (typically nonfunctionally requirements) that are signed as service level agreements (SLAs). They express the users' expectations that all of the software's features will be fully available.

Consider the reverse scenario. If the software isn't available in production, this absence can be detected by monitoring systems or (even worse) by the users themselves. The operations team is then directly blamed for the downtime and its reputation drops. The mixture of responsibility and direct perceptions from external users leads operations to focus on maintaining a stable production environment and its software. Every change to the production environment is risky and a potential cause of disturbance.

The main task of the development team is to fulfill the customer's requirements, test the solution, and provide software updates in quick succession (see Figure 2-2). New features that have been implemented and tested by the developers add potential value for the customer. On the one hand, the development team wants change. On the other hand, the operations team is mainly interested in reliable and stable software. Every change forwarded by the development team can endanger the existing reliability and stability.

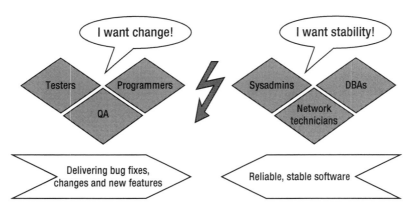

Figure 2-2. *Development (testers, programmers, QA) wants changes. Operations (sysadmins, network technicians, DBAs) wants stability. This misalignment leads to conflicts*

Let's summarize the key findings. Agile primarily improves on the classic approach by introducing the whole team approach, where developers, testers, and QA form a team that closely collaborates with the business. The unified team works as a unit of specialists who simultaneously perform general duties and who share responsibility for producing high-quality software. However, operations is not a part of that team. The misalignment of goals and tasks often results in a blame game, which we'll discuss next.

Blame Game: Dev vs. Ops

What are the effects of a software delivery process on the participants, and why does it lead to conflict? To understand this problem better, we must examine the daily motivations of the key people. As more features are completed, the developer's reputation improves. Throughput and a good velocity are considered to be a reflection of great performance by the developers. In many situations, from the developer's viewpoint, the new features available on test machines will be indistinguishable from the features that are deployed on production systems available for users.

Programmers, testers, database administrators, and system administrators experience challenges every day. These problems include risky or faulty deployments of software, an unnecessarily sluggish delivery process, and suboptimal collaboration and communication due to walls. These issues often lead to an overall slowdown that causes the company to lag behind its competitors and thus be placed at a disadvantage.

Conflicts During Deployment

Conflicts between development and operations teams often originate from time pressures. Typically, a new software release must be deployed quickly. Another scenario that requires operations team to react quickly is when the system is down, and restoring it quickly becomes the highest priority. This situation often leads to a blame game where each side accuses the other of causing the problem.

Common scenarios include the following:

1. Development passes a new release to operations, but the latter is unable to get it running on the production system.

2. The operations team contacts the members of the development team to get them to fix the problem; the former describes the errors experienced while trying to bring the release to production.

3. In response, development blocks communication and does not offer any help.

4. Development claims (correctly) that the software release ran in a test environment without any problems. Therefore, development reasons that the operations team is at fault for not bringing the release to life. Finger pointing from both sides may end in angry phone calls, rancorous e-mails, and even escalation meetings.

5. After escalating the issue to the boss and his or her boss, two engineers are again assigned to look into the malfunction.

6. By investigating both the testing and production environments together, they discover that the two environments are different in some minor detail, such as a technical user or a clustering mode. Neither party knew about this difference.

By discovering the error together and aligning the systems with each other manually, the teams can successfully deploy the new software release to production. Of course, the blame game continues later because each party thinks it was the task of the other side to flag the difference as an issue or to adjust the systems accordingly.

Conflicts After Deployment

The blame game also often emerges when a new release goes live. Here is one scenario:

1. Many more users are using the new features than the company expected.

2. Response times slow down until the software stops responding entirely. The users are panicking because this is the worst-case scenario.

3. Escalating the issue leads to finger pointing: development claims it is the fault of the database group, the database team blames the network group, and others speculate that the server group is responsible for the outage.

4. After going through intensive emotional torture, the company begins an objective examination that finds the root cause of the issue. However, by this point, the users have already been scared away from the new application. As a result, the company incurs heavy losses in sales and reputation.

Conflicts About Performance

The blame game can also occur in the following scenario:

1. A performance issue suddenly happens in the production system.

2. Following a blame game, the developers identify an issue in the application. They work long days before finally providing a patch that fixes the issue.

3. Nonetheless, the operations team is still annoyed by the performance issue and is reminded of similar instances in the past, where every subsequent patch further reduced the stability of the software. As a result, the operations team is leery of applying the patch.

4. The team members suggest coding the software themselves because of those problems. This suggestion, in turn, heightens the emotional tension between the teams. The operations team wants the patch to be applied in a test environment to ensure that it does not infect the overall stability of the application and that it actually fixes the performance bottleneck.

5. Unfortunately, the test environment does not fully mirror the production environment, and there are no test scenarios or test data that can imitate the exact same problem on the test machine. Days and weeks go by, and the patch is still not applied to production. All those long days spent working on the solution were for naught.

6. The management and business units increase the pressure to solve the problem, the development and operations teams continue their conflict, all are frustrated, and the performance issue on the production machine is not solved.

Unfortunately, these horror stories are common (although not necessarily the rule). Have you experienced these types of scenarios? Did you come to the conclusion that, in retrospect, it would have been much better (and much faster) to work on the solution together from the start?

Project life is hard, and many conflicts may arise between development and operations. However, it is possible to narrow down these problems. The core issue responsible for most of the conflicts between operations and development is that the operations department is often considered to be a bottleneck. We'll address this perception in the next section.

Operations as Bottleneck

Many teams and projects focus on the blame game and the daily burdens of delivering software. The conflict between development and operations worsened when development began adopting more Agile processes while developing software. Processes such as Scrum (a management framework that supports iterative and incremental Agile software development) suggest holistic approaches that bring together businesspeople and development and release increments every two to four weeks. During the past few years, these iterative models have become mainstream, but all too often, companies have stopped adding people and activities to the Scrum process at the point when software releases were shipped to production.

■ **Note** Please keep in mind that this book primarily targets developers. Be aware of the fact that *developers* comprise more than testers, programmers, and experts for QA; rather, the one team approach (as introduced in this book) also includes experts from operations who develop, for instance, scripts or "infrastructure as code" to provide solutions to users.

The advantages of Agile processes, including Scrum and Kanban (a method for delivering software with an emphasis on just-in-time delivery, see Chapter 6), are often nullified because of the obstacles to collaboration, processes, and tools that are built up in front of operations. As a result, software is released frequently but only in test environments. Consequently, software is rarely brought to the production phase, which transforms a new release into a solution and provides value to the end user and to the customer. In other words, not all releases are produced, and deployment to production often happens after the development team has coded and tested the release. In sum, the cycle time (i.e., the time from the inception of an idea to its delivery to users) is still too long. High frequency of software releases from development and the incentives (and its implications) for operations lead to what many people in the company will perceive as a bottleneck at operations.

Development wants operations to bring their changes to production, but operations may be reluctant to accept release calendars that are too quick on the trigger (often because of negative experience such as unstable applications; trust must often be earned again in small steps). As a result, development may have finished the functionality in fast cycles by using Agile frameworks such as Scrum, but operations may not want or be unable to receive all of the changes in these fine-grained portions. Operations provides some release slots where new (or changed) functionalities can be passed to production (see Figure 2-3). As you can imagine, these different views on software releases aren't fully congruent.

 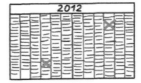

Completed functions   Release weekends

Figure 2-3. *A heavy mismatch between the viewpoints of the development team, which wants to bring frequent changes to the user, and the operations team, which offers dedicated slots for bringing software to production*[2]

However, from the development team's viewpoint, the wait time for the release slot is not the only problem. Another issue is that this release slot is time-boxed, which means that the new software version must "go live" in a concrete time interval (e.g., during one day). If problems occur during these short intervals, it's not always possible to find solutions, and in the worst-case scenario, the operations team rolls back to the old version of the software, and the development department is given some additional tasks that they have to consider for their next opportunity (i.e., the next release slot) sometime in the future. Development will blame operations for not being able or willing to set the software live. Operations will blame the development team members because of their inability to develop production-ready software.

The root cause of these mismatches can be narrowed down to different goals and suboptimal collaboration between these groups. The underlying cause is also influenced by the horizontal alignment, which is covered in the next section.

Horizontal Optimization

The horizontal optimization approach implies a limited amount of usable infrastructure components[3] and therefore a reduced set of options when choosing the perfect architecture. Here, operations has the higher priority, and possible synergies are found and applied through, for example, load balancing techniques, reductions in the number of different system topologies, or the necessary skills of the team members. The horizontal optimization approach focuses on utilizing architecture components, as shown in Figure 2-4.

The horizontal optimization method is preferred by operations. With this approach, the operations department can optimize its utilization of infrastructure components as well as its service management. In companies, operations is often a part of information technology (IT) service management efforts. We'll discuss this concept next.

Operations and ITSM

Operations can be integrated into IT service management (ITSM) (see Figure 2-5). ITSM involves the organization's management of its processes and its delivery of IT services to its users. For most companies, their view of ITSM begins and ends at the service desk, but it

---

[2] My thanks to Udo Pracht for the idea of this figure.
[3] Also the operations team may be limited in the sense that projects may compete for the time of the experts from the operations team.

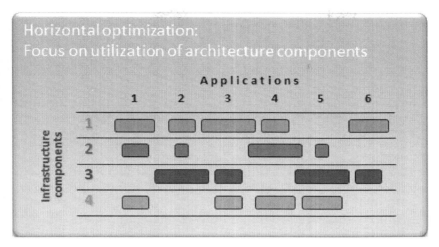

Figure 2-4. *Agile software development spans the process from inception to transition. DevOps spans the process from elaboration to operations[4]*

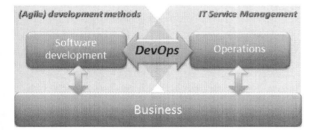

Figure 2-5. *DevOps links software development to operations. Both are based on business. Software development is influenced by Agile methods, whereas operations is influenced by service management[5]*

actually encompasses much more than the company's services. Instead, to support a service across operations and the business unit, ITSM requires greater collaboration around the provision of resources.

Although operations has certain alignments with business, it is often heavily driven by service management and the optimization of infrastructure management. With DevOps, Agile approaches are applied to operations in addition to development. We cover the scope of DevOps in the next section.

---

[4] My thanks to Udo Pracht for the idea of this figure.
[5] My thanks to Udo Pracht for the idea of this figure.

DevOps to the Rescue

In the past few years, many people have worked to apply Agile approaches to operations. Those approaches aimed to eliminate the wall between development and operations and to address the structural conflict between those two departments. By sharing experiences and possible solutions, the movement formed into what is now called DevOps. The processes by which the movement formed itself and discussed and provided solutions to the pain points summarized above are similar to how the Agile movement started its work years ago. From another perspective, DevOps aims to extend Agile to operations.

DEVOPS ONE TEAM APPROACH: DEVELOPMENT AND OPERATIONS

With the DevOps approach, the developer role consists of programmers, testers, QA, and experts from operations. They all develop software and help to bring it to the user.

The comparison of tasks and views of development and operations shows that the two teams have different goals and incentives and that these differences lead to conflict. Development strives for change (e.g., new features and bug fixes), whereas the operations team strives for stability. Often, those groups are paid precisely for these tasks: development obtains bonus payments if the software is delivered, whereas operations is rewarded if production systems are stable. Thus, the development department desires a high flow of newly provided functionality, whereas the operations department prefers to avoid putting any new release into production.

Both teams follow their respective goals by focusing on their individual tasks and by fulfilling their obligations to obtain positive attention from management and visibility for doing a great job. To achieve their respective goals, development and operations often use their own processes and tools. The sets of processes and tools are optimized locally (for each group) to obtain the best local result.

Although these approaches are great from their isolated viewpoints, the total flow of software is reduced, and the overall project (or company) goal is thwarted. As a result, silos are constructed, conflicts exist on a daily basis, and people are working against one another instead of with one another to provide the best solution possible.[6]

The Essence of DevOps

A core ideal of the DevOps movement is that both well-known and new approaches, processes, and tools can be summarized. Although this diversity may lead to different opinions about what is part of DevOps, many different aspects may also be included under the DevOps label. This feature benefits communication considerably because experts from different disciplines can relate to DevOps and bring their individual experiences and skill together under the DevOps label. By being grouped together, these experts can more easily enter discussions and share their knowledge and experience with one another. A term such as DevOps causes management

---

[6] Steve Jobs used to say, "Real artists ship."

to pay attention to the DevOps concept and the fact that development and operations need to collaborate to find synergies and develop a competitive advantage.

In the following, I'll explain the essence of DevOps by starting with the shared values and goals.

Values and Goals

Similar to the Agile movement, DevOps has a strong focus on interpersonal aspects. DevOps is about putting the fun back into IT! However, what does collaboration mean? There are many prerequisites to cooperation and trust, including the following:

- Respect for one another.

- Commitment to shared goals.

- Collective ownership.

- Shared values.

Essential to improving collaboration is the alignment of incentives across teams as well as the application of shared processes and tools. The main attributes of aligned incentives include a shared definition of quality for the whole project or company and a commitment to it. Aligned with defined quality attributes, visibility and transparency can help to foster collaboration. Incentives must treat the development and operations groups as one team. That is, they should be rewarded for developing many changes that are stable and shipped.

This structure can end the rift between the two groups, which are all too often rewarded in conflicting ways, as discussed above. Rewarding some for innovation and others for stability inherently creates conflict. Rewarding everyone for stable innovations fosters collaboration. As a prerequisite, teams are cross-functional. The team includes programmers, testers, QA, and operations. Thus, individual experts share their skills and experiences with others, which leads to a one team approach where individuals have at least a basic understanding of others' domains (see Figure 2-6).

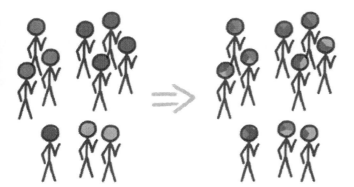

Figure 2-6. *DevOps leads to teams that bring together experts who share their skills and experiences. All experts have at least a basic understanding of the others' business subjects*[7]

---

[7] My thanks to Udo Pracht for the idea of this figure.

DevOps is about team play and a collaborative problem-solving approach. If a service goes down, everyone must know what procedures to follow to diagnose the problem and get the system up and running again. Additionally, all of the roles and skills necessary to perform these tasks must be available and able to work together well. Training and effective collaboration are critical here.

Because of the changing requirements for team members, DevOps will gain more importance in central companies, such as human relations, which has to hire people who are open-minded and willing to collaborate in a team.

Processes

Processes that define how software is developed and delivered are more important than tools. After developing a process that fits your individual requirements and basic conditions, you can choose the tools that best implement your process. Processes are even more important when addressing the interactions between different departments. A handover of artifacts for delivery must be defined. Does that mean we have to merge development and operations into one department? No. It's more important to install interdisciplinary experts in the interface of both development and operations.

Later in this book, we'll discuss patterns describing how to accomplish the following:

- Aligning responsibilities with artifacts (deliverables), not with roles (the latter is the traditional approach).

- Setting up and streamlining a holistic process that maintains speed while development hands off software to operations.

- Including development and operations in a comprehensive end-to-end delivery process.

- Including operations in Agile frameworks and processes, such as Scrum and Kanban.

Development and operations share the same processes, and both groups are focused on delivering application changes to the user at a high frequency and quality. The unified process emphasizes the cycle time and prefers the vertical optimization approach. According to this method, every application is created and executed on the architecture that is perfect for this concrete application (see Figure 2-7). The individual components of the infrastructure are laid out to fulfill the requirements for the specific application. Optimization across the borders of individual applications is rare or does not occur at all. Thus, synergies while administrating applications do not have a high priority.

Traditionally, the vertical optimization approach is preferred by the development team. In DevOps, both development and operations prefer workable solutions in production and are open-minded about optimizing vertically.

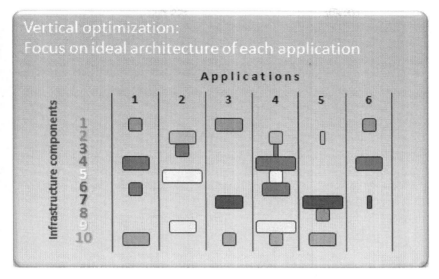

Figure 2-7. *Vertical optimization is aligned with individual solutions and focuses on the ideal architectures of each application*[8]

Tools

Processes are more important than tools, but tools are still important, especially for automating activities along the delivery process. The more tools you have in your tool kit, the better you can decide which tool is the best fit for a given task.

Streamlining DevOps is heavily reliant on end-to-end automation. Consider all of the steps in a build. These steps include preparing the build system; applying baselines to source control systems; conducting the build; running technical, functional, and acceptance tests; packing; and deploying and staging the artifacts. All are automated with the appropriate tools. Code and scripts are stored in version control systems. Code and scripts for DevOps include the following:

- Code and scripts for building the application.

- Code and scripts for unit testing the application.

- Code and scripts for acceptance testing the application.

- Code and scripts for deploying the application.

- Code and script configuration options for configuring the application for different target environments.

- Code and scripts for programming the attributes and "behavior" of the target environment.

---

[8] My thanks to Udo Pracht for the idea of this figure.

The last point is of great interest. With tools like Puppet or Chef (which we will discuss later), domain-specific languages (DSL) can be used to describe the attributes of the environment (e.g., technical users, permissions, and installed packages). The code and scripts are stored in the version control system, such as Git (a distributed version control system) or Subversion (a centralized version control system). This approach has many benefits, including the following:

- Abstracted descriptions of machines by using a DSL while enjoying the full power of scripting languages (in both Puppet and Chef, you can describe behavior in the Ruby language (a dynamic, general-purpose object-oriented programming language), see http://www.ruby-lang.org/en/).

- Declarative descriptions of target behavior (i.e., what the system must be). Thus, running the scripts will always lead to the same end result.

- Management of code in version control. By using a version control system as the leading medium, you do not need to adjust the machines manually (which is not reproducible).

- Synchronization of environments by using a version control system and automatic provisioning of environments. Continuous integration servers, such as Jenkins, simply have to listen to the path in the version control system to detect changes. Then the configuration management tool (e.g., Puppet) ensures that the corresponding machines apply the behavior that is described in version control.

- Using tools such as Jenkins (see Chapter 8) and Puppet and Vagrant (see Chapter 9), complete setups, including virtualizations, can be managed automatically.

- Sharing of scripts (e.g., Puppet manifests). A cross-functional team that includes development and operations can develop this function.

Sharing the scripts in the version control system enables all parties, particularly development and operations, to use those scripts to set up their respective environments: test environments (used by development) and production environments (managed by operations).

Automation is an essential backbone of DevOps (see Chapter 3 and Chapter 8 for more information on automation). Automation is the use of solutions to reduce the need for human work. Automation can ensure that the software is built the same way each time, that the team sees every change made to the software, and that the software is tested and reviewed in the same way every day so that no defects slip through or are introduced through human error.

In software development projects, a high level of automation is a prerequisite for quickly delivering the best quality and for obtaining feedback from stakeholders early and often. Automating aspects of DevOps helps to make parts of the process transparent for the whole team and also helps deploy software to different target environments in the same way. You can best improve what you measure; and to measure something usefully, you need a process that delivers results in a reproducible way.

DevOps addresses aspects similar to those tackled by Agile development, but the former focuses on breaking down the walls between developers and operations workers. The challenge is to communicate the benefits of DevOps to both development and operations teams. Both groups may be reluctant to start implementing the shift toward DevOps because their day is already full of activities. So why should they be concerned with the work of others? Why should operations want to use unfamiliar tools and adjust their daily routines when their self-made, isolated solutions have worked just fine for years?

Because of this resistance, the incentives and commitment provided by upper management are important. Incentives alone are not enough: unified processes and tool chains are also important. Upper management will also resist by questioning the wisdom of implementing DevOps if the concrete benefits are not visible. Better cash flow and improved time to market are hard to measure. Management asks questions that address the core problems of software engineering while ignoring the symptoms: how can the company achieve maximal earnings in a short period of time? How can requirements be made stable and delivered to customers quickly? These results and visions should be measured with metrics that are shared by development and operations. Existing metrics can be further used or replaced by metrics that accurately express business value. One example of an end-to-end metric is the cycle time, which we will discuss in detail in Chapter 3.

Conclusion

In this chapter, we've taken the long journey from classic project settings to the DevOps approach. In the past, Agile approaches successfully addressed common obstacles between programmers, testers, QA, and customers, but conflicts still remained. We've identified the conflicts between development and operations that have often led to silos and suboptimal solutions. The blame game between development and operations often occurs, which shows the conflicts produced by divergent goals, processes, and tools.

Extending Agile approaches to operations can result in the one team approach, which also includes operations in Agile. Both development and operations profit from Agile approaches. Development and operations work hand in hand, with shared goals, processes, and tools.

DevOps can serve as a label for many different aspects of software engineering. In a discussion of DevOps, it can be helpful to slice DevOps into three perspectives: shared goals, processes, and tools. The combination of these perspectives comprises the essence of DevOps.

In the next chapter, we'll explore the building blocks of DevOps. We'll discover that the cycle time is a crucial metric that has relevance for all stakeholders.

Building Blocks of DevOps

To estimate project duration we apply Celsius to Fahrenheit formula. C is internal estimate and F is what we tell PM: C × 9/5 + 32 = F days.

—DevOps Borat[1]

In this chapter, we'll examine the building blocks of DevOps. We'll talk about the metrics, and you'll learn that the cycle time is the most important metric for both development and operations. We'll also discuss how to improve and accelerate software delivery. Let's start with measurement and metrics.

Measurement and Metrics

A crucial aspect of software engineering is measuring what you are doing. Sooner or later, you'll have to decide on which metrics you want to use during your software engineering process. You'll have to consider which metric is meaningful enough to aid all participants, as well as the development and delivery processes.

Traditional projects emphasize measurement as an important tool for tracking progress, identifying the current status, and scheduling dates. Agile project settings try to find different approaches to create measurements, but often find themselves on dead-end streets when trying to bridge operations to development. Both traditional and Agile projects often emphasize the importance of measurement because you can only improve if you measure. Let's take a brief look at how traditional projects understand measurement and metrics.

---

[1]http://twitter.com/devops_borat/status/111854984852811776.

Traditional Use of Metrics

Classic metrics are often driven by numbers: they try to summarize and aggregate highly complex dependencies into single numbers. Counting leads to the illusion that we can understand something because we can quantify it. Have you encountered PowerPoint slides that provide one single number to illustrate the status of the project (e.g., cost effectiveness, capacity utilization[2], or meeting target scope, all in percentages)? Numbers suggest the illusion of control. However, numbers can be very misleading. Worse, counting all too often leads to perverse incentives. Even if managers are not assessing people based on process metrics, counting things affects behavior.

■ **Note** In classic projects, extensive measurement and metrics are often used to "manage by the numbers."

Classic metrics, such as static code analysis or test coverage, may continuously draw the attention of the whole team without returning benefits in the same degree. It is simply too easy to fake metrics or to adapt the process to obey the metrics instead of improving the process itself (e.g., adding empty test bodies or commenting out broken tests to optimize the test coverage metric).

Conservative approaches that use "function points" to determine functionality can be misleading as well. You may measure the output of software development by using "functions points" to measure functionality, but you cannot derive the real value or any productivity from them.

Traditional metrics are often abused to compare teams or individuals. The best way to mess up the usefulness of any process metric is to use it to judge people. For example, if a manager uses the velocity or the number of defects to compare teams, the manager will have a serious problem.

■ **Note** Velocity is a metric that provides information about the "rate of progress" for the team. For example, velocity can be the number of user stories a team can perform in one interval, where it is important to include testing and shipping in the measure. Thus, a short form could be represented as "running tested features" (RTF).[3]

Agile Approach to Metrics

Agile development methods require a disciplined approach to ensure that customer feedback, continuous testing, and iterative development actually lead to frequent deliveries of working, valuable software.

Software applications consist of functionality, and in many cases, new features will be created continuously. Only features that ship add value and form and improve upon a "solution."

---

[2]Different approaches for measuring capacity are discussed by John Allspaw in his book *The Art of Capacity Planning* (O'Reilly, 2008).
[3]See http://xprogramming.com/xpmag/jatRtsMetric.

A solution is more than a mere set of features; a solution is an application that adds value to and benefits the user (the person using the application) or the customer (the person with the money).

Agile often discusses value instead of specific metrics and points out that software must be shipped to customers to be valuable. Specified (but not implemented) and implemented (but not shipped) software is often considered waste because time and money was invested to specify and build the software without obtaining any return. As a result, nothing is delivered that would help the user to work more efficiently or improve the company's competitive advantage against other companies in the market.

Agile development teams often view metrics as a onetime pointer instead of a continuous measurement. The pointer makes the current state of the software's internal quality visible. It is then up to the team to decide when to adjust the code base or whether to do so at all. These pointers provide indicators that there's something worth investigating, but they don't provide the context and understanding needed to make critical decisions.

Definition of Done

Another well-known and commonly used approach is the Definition of Done (DoD). Before the job is started, the definition of a completed job is specified, and the team commits to this definition. DoD often states that no development job is finished until testing is complete or the software is shipped to target systems, in a defined quality, or that monitoring is available for shipped software. By using DoD, the whole team shares the same understanding of when the task is completed. Additionally, DoD requires new features to add value to the system and to the customer after it has been shipped and made available to him or her.

Broken Agile Metrics

Despite good intentions, metrics are often broken in Agile teams. The following are some examples of broken metrics:

- *Test pass/fail ratios*: The Agile team stops the line and immediately fixes a broken test. Thus, the test pass/fail ratio is not useful because the team stops and directly fixes the regression. However, the metric is useful for detecting basic flaws. For example, if the test coverage is below 20 percent, it is pretty obvious that technical debt has been accumulated.

■ **Note** Technical debt is a metaphor to describe the eventual consequences of suboptimal software. The debt is open work that needs to be done before a task can be considered completed.

- *Number of defects created or resolved*: What information can you extract from the number of defects created or tickets resolved? Instead of helping to move the project forward, these numbers too often result in finger pointing and arguing about what was and wasn't a bug or a feature. As Figure 3-1 shows, having information about new and closed tickets or the history of the amount of tickets does not provide information about the application itself or how much value a new feature will return.

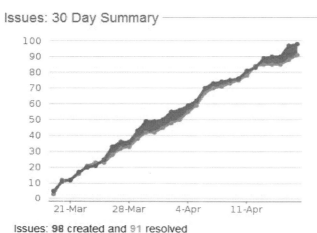

Issues: 30 Day Summary

Issues: **98** created and **91** resolved

Figure 3-1. *A ticket system often shows some data and curves about created and resolved tickets. This information is certainly interesting but not as meaningful as it initially appears.*

- *Continuous deployments*: Deployment processes that, at least in theory, continuously build, package, and deploy the software that is up and running. However, build jobs are often broken, and packaged applications frequently cannot be deployed to a target system. Obviously, there is a gap between what the application expects of the target environment and the current state of that environment, the deploy scripts are faulty, or the process is not described at all. Clearly, all of these problems are not ideal.

RELEASE AND DEPLOYMENT

A release is a specific software version that you make available to users. A release is created by promoting a specific release candidate. A release candidate is more than an arbitrary version of the software. A release candidate already has fulfilled specific requirements (e.g., all tests run successfully). Deployment occurs if you install a release (or even a release candidate or a version) of your software into a particular environment.

Some interesting mixes may evolve as well. For example, if a traditional manager tries to institute the notion of a personal velocity on an Agile team, the manager will definitely need some coaching. Being blind to the implications of personal goals, such as a better personal velocity, is dangerous. People don't help one another because they know their own personal productivity would decline if they spent their time helping others. Alternatively, they will not help if it appears that the colleague will perform better after receiving help from another colleague.

Other metrics do not mirror the goals of individuals; rather, they mirror the goals of groups. Often severe incidents and the response time needed to address these incidents are measured. As you can imagine, those approaches are often orthogonal: software development focuses on the internal quality of the software or its external quality (that is, in short, the delivered sum of functionality), whereas operations focuses on the runtime properties of applications or even complete servers. Thus, we need different approaches to measurement and metrics to streamline development and operations. However, let's first discuss changes in software.

Qualify Changes

Agile teams often do not distinguish between bugs, enhancements, or change requests. They use a general unit called change to track progress. Change seems to be a valid unit for both development and operations because operations teams primarily think in terms of changes to the production system. Using changes as a shared term for both development and operations makes it easier to stream production issues back to a work backlog (that is ideally shared by both groups).

Thinking about a change leads to follow-up questions. How much change is generated and transported to operations? What type of change do we have in a particular situation, and how often is a change applied?

As soon as a change is applied to the system, it may lead to a problem. It takes a significant amount of time to notice the problem and to identify its root cause. After some further investigation, you'll have to decide whether to roll back to an older version to fix the problem or roll forward by applying a fix or at least a workaround (i.e., to fix the problem at some future point in time; see Figure 3-2).

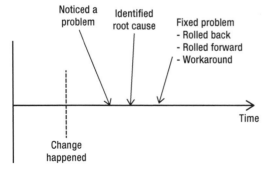

Figure 3-2. *Reducing different change types to simply change can serve as the basis for cooperation between development and operations. After a change occurs, it may result in problems. The problem is noticed, identified, and resolved.*

MTTR AND MTTD

Operations often use the terms mean time to repair/resolve (MTTR), which refers to the time it takes to resolve a system or network issue (after a technician receives a trouble ticket) and restore normal operations following an incident, and mean time to detect (MTTD), which describes the difference between the onset of the incident in production and its detection by the operations team who then initiates a specific action to recover the event back to its original state. A guaranteed MTTR is often defined as part of a service-level agreement (SLA). For more information about MTTR and MTTD see "Web Operations: Keeping the Data On Time", by John Allspaw, Jesse Robbins, O'Reilly, 2010, pages 82-87.

Why not consider all changes to a system, including changes in software, middleware, and infrastructure, as change? Doing so may improve the shared understanding between development and operations. Confidence must be raised so that change is viewed not as an outage but as a normal process (see Table 3-1).

Table 3-1. *Types of Changes that Arise in Software Engineering*

Layers	Example
Application code	Java code, deployment descriptors, build scripts
Middleware	Apache, MySQL, PHP, configuration files
Infrastructure	Operating system, servers, switches, routers

Given that a "change" can serve as a shared unit of measurement, let's now explore what the cycle time can contribute to the process.

Improving Flow of Features

DevOps is essentially about gaining fast feedback and decreasing the risk of releases through a holistic approach that is meaningful for both development and operations. One major step for achieving this approach is to improve the flow of features from their inception to availability. This process can be refined to the point that it becomes important to reduce batch size (the size of one package of changes or the amount of work that is done before the new version is shipped) without changing capacity or demand. On that note, I define some key terms here.

Cycle Time

The cycle time is the period required to complete one cycle of an operation, function, or process. The cycle time required to process a customer order might start with the customer's phone call and end with the order being shipped. In software engineering, cycle time describes the amount of time required from the start of the development process to the beginning of revenue generation. The overall process comprises many different steps. The cumulative cycle time of all of the subprocesses in your operation determines when you can promise a delivered feature to your customer. Cycle time is only meaningful if you define "done" as the point at which the features have been developed, tested, and shipped to the customer, who can then begin using them.

Donald G. Reinertsen discusses this concept in his books[4] He decomposes cycle time into three pieces: the Fuzzy Front End (FFE), the development cycle, and time-to-volume. The FFE begins at the earliest point in time at which one could have started working on the project. Often, the date on which a written project proposal form is submitted is used.

The end of the FFE is marked with the opening of a charge number to start collecting the costs of development. This act normally signifies that the company is seriously pursuing the product. This signal marks the beginning of what we might call the development cycle. The development cycle ends with the first revenue-producing shipment of the product. The final phase, time-to-volume, ends if all project objectives have been completed. Objectives often include achieving target quality goals and delivering enough volume to satisfy demand. Until these goals are met, the work of the development team will not end because economic opportunities will remain. If you declare victory as soon as the product ships, then there is likely to be insufficient attention devoted to the residual engineering that must be performed to finish optimizing the product for production. Insisting that all of this optimization takes place before shipping the first unit is usually a bad economic choice, albeit a common mistake.

It can be useful to define cycle time differently in other situations, but the key point is to agree on a measurable starting point and a measurable endpoint.

It's important to understand that cycle time supports a holistic approach in software engineering that spans different departments and project roles. The cycle time can serve as a key metric shared by development and operations. There are other terms in use, too, that you'll learn next.

Lead Time, Takt Time, and Throughput

The term *lead time* can be used in addition to cycle time. For instance, lead time can refer to the amount of time between an input for a request to the system and the completion of that order. Lead time typically includes queuing time and work order preparation time. Therefore, in product development, I would include both the FFE and development cycle when measuring lead time.

Takt time is primarily a manufacturing term that refers to the rhythm of the process. I don't use this term often because I prefer to refer to the cadence of a process, such as the release of code every 24 hours. Usually, manufacturing will refer to a single takt time for a process, such as the production of one car off a line every five minutes. If the takt time changes this timing, the change is propagated to all subprocesses. I prefer to refer to cadence because I can specify that to a weekly deployment cadence and a daily testing cadence.

Some people may use terms in different ways. For example, the term *throughput* is used to refer to both the quantity of output and the output rate. Thus, it is helpful to set up a glossary in your project to ensure a common understanding of key terms.

---

[4]See *Developing Products in Half the Time* (Wiley, 1997) and *The Principles of Product Development Flow: Second Generation Lean Product Development* (Celeritas, 2009).

Improve and Accelerate Delivery

How can the cycle time help to reduce batch size? If we reduce batch size, we can deploy more frequently because reducing batch size drives down cycle time. After a release engineering team spends a weekend in a data center deploying the past three months' worth of work, the last thing anybody wants to do is deploy again anytime soon. If a task is painful, the solution is to do it more often and bring the pain forward. As Figure 3-3 shows, choosing small releases over big releases eventually delivers the same amount of functionality, but more functionality is delivered much more quickly, and the software will return value more quickly.

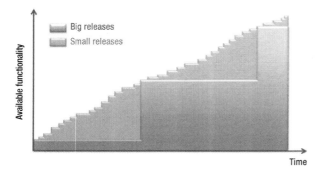

Figure 3-3. *By using big releases, you will have large batch sizes, and functionality will be shipped late. By using small releases, you will use appropriate batch sizes, and functionality will be available much sooner.*

Deploying to production frequently will help keep things simple and make the individual changes more focused. The risk of deployments is reduced because you practice the process of deployment. By bringing the pain forward, you'll identify problems in your process and tool chains earlier and will be able to optimize accordingly. As a result, the deployment itself will also only change in smaller batches between different deployments.

Another big advantage of deploying to production frequently is that the process of fixing incidents will become optimized too.

Deploying more frequently means that changes between deployments are small, and that in turn helps with learning about the root causes of production incidents and getting the production system back up again. Uncovering your errors becomes much easier because the amount of change is much smaller. Once uncovered, errors can be fixed faster, and that makes a total rollback unnecessary.

Deploying frequently will not only reduce the needs for rolling back to past versions of your software, but even if you have to roll back, you only need to roll back a small set of changes, which is much easier technically than rolling back a release that contains the total work of months or years. Rolling back is not only a technical issue; but it's also more manageable from a business viewpoint (e.g., customer satisfaction or marketing activities) to roll back single features than to roll back a full release with hundreds of features.

If your deployment pipeline is truly efficient, it's often quicker to check in a forward rolling change (e.g., a bug fix in the code) instead of working with cumbersome rollbacks. Always applying changes to create new versions of the software (meaning always rolling forward) has the direct advantage that your deployment process is more focused and simpler, because you don't need to set up and maintain an often complex rollback process.

Thus, increasing the change frequency and decreasing the respective change sizes (see Figure 3-4) can generate many advantages.

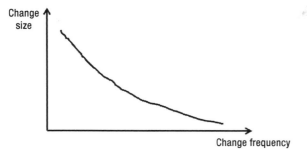

Figure 3-4. *Changes occur often, but the amount of each respective change is smaller and thus less risky, more convenient, and quicker to the market.*

Automatic Releasing

Many risk reduction practices exist, such as continuous integration and automatic tests. On a higher level, these practices can be summarized as recipes for releasing. There is functional releasing (assigning and tracking work items to target releases) and technical releasing, which forms baselines ("known good" states), a consistent and versioned set of configuration items. Automatic releasing is the practice of creating releases (or at least release candidates) automatically. One key goal of automatic releasing is to reduce the risk of releasing software. An effective strategy for automatic releasing can reduce the risk of any individual release. In the following, we'll explore some general ideas that make automatic releasing efficient.

Automating common tasks in building, testing (see Chapters 4 and 10), and releasing (see Chapter 8) software helps to increase efficiency and set up a reproducible process that can be implemented by tool chains. We can even automate the provisioning and deployment of the virtual machines and middleware (see Chapter 9), and application code. This automation ensures repeatability. In my book *Agile ALM*,[5] I stated that "automating the integration, build, packaging, and deployment steps will facilitate rapid iterative development" and that "automating the most error-prone, most repetitive, and most time-consuming activities is essential."

Pitfalls of Automation

Should you automate 100 percent of everything? In the following sections, I illustrate four aspects that are of interest while automating common tasks. These aspects are not obvious, but ignoring their relevance can generate ugly results.

---

[5]Hüttermann, *Agile ALM: Lightweight Tools and Agile Strategies* (Shelter Island, N.Y.: Manning, 2011), p. 71.

Law of Marginal Costs

In most cases, you should not automate everything, although some people strive for full auto-mation. Full automation is often impossible and does not make sense from a business perspec-tive. Consider the law of marginal costs. The software under development needs maintenance, and enhancements are coded continuously. The same is true for the (automation) system itself. If something has to change in the running (automation) system because new requirements have emerged or changes are being implemented (in both cases, the automation system and the application itself may result in changes in the automation system), these activities will cost time and thus money. Running an automation system costs money. Obvious examples include test and build scripts.

Verb/Noun Mistake

Additionally, project activities are often mixed up with sense and stateless deliverables (i.e., the "verb/noun mistake"). Let's again consider the testing discipline. Testing is an activity (i.e., it's not a noun). Understanding testing as a noun is suboptimal and may lead to a focus on mean-ingless artifact types (e.g., test cases) instead of concretely and effectively testing the applica-tion. So you will most probably not want to automate 100 percent of your tests just to have a big batch of test cases. Moreover, a crucial part of tests cannot be automated at all (e.g., exploratory testing of user interfaces). This limitation applies to other disciplines as well.

Paradox of Automation

Another aspect that should be considered is the "paradox of automation." The paradox of auto-mation[6] says that "the more efficient the automated system is, the more essential the human contribution that is needed to run the automation system. Humans are less involved in heavily automated systems, but their involvement becomes more critical." If an automated system has an error, the full system is often completely unavailable until the error is identified (first chal-lenge) and fixed (second challenge). Finding the error is a nontrivial task that cannot be per-formed by a novice engineer who is not an expert at the underlying, automated baby steps. Even if you have the confidence to claim that a problem does not exist because the system runs at the moment, there are always scenarios (besides the nice weather scenario) that provoke malfunc-tions or errors in this running system. Strong skills and experience are needed to monitor and operate a (running) system. Additionally, strong skills and experience are required to maintain and develop the system further because requirements will change and new requirements will be raised in the future.

Irony of Automation

The final aspect is the "irony of automation." "The more reliable the plant, the less opportunity there will be for the operator to practice direct intervention, and the more difficult will be the demands of the remaining tasks requiring operator intervention."[7]

---

[6]http://book.personalmba.com/paradox-of-automation/.

[7]Josh Kaufman, http://www.bainbrdg.demon.co.uk/Papers/Ironies.html.

According to Ashwin Parameswaran, running most scenarios via "autopilot" with a high automation grade results in a deskilled and novice human operator who cannot fix the system if it fails. In his essay "People Make Poor Monitors for Computers," he claims "Because a failure is inevitably taken as evidence of human failure, the system is automated even further, and more safeguards and redundancies are built into the system. This increased automation exacerbates the absence of feedback if small errors occur. The buildup of latent errors again increases, and failures become even more catastrophic."[8]

As a possible consequence from accidents in highly automated systems (see for example the reports about the Three Mile Island accident[9]), you may claim that only the error situation itself provides a situation you can learn from to improve and do better. But as soon as the incident arises, it may be too late to adjust accordingly. An interesting way to address that could be to introduce predetermined breaking points into the automation system in order to reduce the automation grade to less than is technically possible. If part of a human operator's daily job is to solve less than critical issues, the same people will be much better prepared to solve very rare critical issues. With this approach, the operator will gain and preserve a better understanding not only about the whole automated system, but also about the single modules and facets that are part of it. This results in the operator becoming what he or she should be: an expert, not a monitor for a computer (for monitoring with tools like Nagios).

Automation Good Practices

In summary, do not automate simply because you want to automate. It's bad if your automation activities are driven by technical instead of business considerations. These activities must result in concrete benefits. Automation is not a discipline in itself. Automation is performed to gain fast feedback. Think about the "verbs" and the "marginal costs." Efficient automation makes humans more important, not less important. Always be aware of the consequences of automation, including the law of marginal costs and the paradox of automation.

Apply Releases Incrementally and Iteratively

Any reasonably mature organization will have production systems composed of several inter-linked components or services, with dependencies between those components. For example, my application might depend on some static content, a database, and some services provided by other systems.

INCREMENTS AND ITERATIONS

"An iteration is a mini-project that may result in an increment of the software. Iterating starts with an idea of what is wanted, and the code is refined to get the desired result. An increment is a small unit of functionality. Incrementing allows you to build a better understanding of what you need, assembling the software piece by piece" (Hüttermann, *Agile ALM*, p. 37).

---

[8] See http://www.macroresilience.com/2011/12/29/people-make-poor-monitors-for-computers/.
[9] http://en.wikipedia.org/wiki/Three_Mile_Island_accident.

Upgrading all of those components in one big-bang release is the highest-risk way of rolling out new functionality. Instead, I would deploy the components independently in a side-by-side configuration wherever possible. For example, if you need to roll out new static content, don't overwrite the old content. Instead, deploy that content in a new directory such that it's accessible via a different uniform resource identifier before you deploy the new version of the application that requires it.

Applying releases incrementally and iteratively helps to streamline your process and to release software automatically. Let's look at how monitoring is another crucial part of DevOps.

Apply Monitoring, Thoroughly

Automatic releasing should be accompanied by monitoring. Monitoring is the activity of continuously collecting and storing data about the state of the application, middleware, and infrastructure and making this state visible to the whole team.

Monitoring is used to detect (or even prevent) production incidents and to minimize MTTR and MTTD. Monitoring can be applied to many different areas and often focuses on availability (e.g., network, processes, ports) and capacity (e.g., memory usage by time interval).

You should not think of monitoring as an isolated down-streamed task. Instead, with DevOps, you should develop the software application and the monitoring solution side by side. By aligning development of monitoring (meaning setting up monitoring and extending the solution continuously) with the development of the whole solution (implementing functional and nonfunctional requirements, building up application, middleware, infrastructure), you will be able to improve monitoring continuously, catch gaps in monitoring early, and ensure that monitoring is always aligned with the concrete needs. Adding monitoring to the Definition of Done for new features of the software application is often a good idea. Patrick Debois even suggests "monitoring-driven development" that comprises creating a monitor check before implementing a feature.[10]

Monitoring can serve as a central vehicle in tracking the process and the maturity of the development. Monitoring often goes in conjunction with smoke testing. Smoke tests are designed to ensure that the deployment was successful and, in particular, to test that the configuration settings (such as the database connection parameter) for the production environment are correct. Smoke tests ensure that your application is basically running after it has been deployed. They may, for example, use automated scripts to launch the application and check that the main pages are generating the expected content or that basic navigation steps on the graphical user interface (GUI) can be fulfilled. Additionally, smoke tests check whether any services that your application depends on (e.g., databases, message buses and third-party systems) are up and running. Similar to monitoring, smoke tests enable fast feedback, and their results should be made visible to the whole team.

DevOps fosters visibility and emphasizes testing. Applications should be tested during their development, thoroughly. But once applications are deployed to production, testing should not stop. Instead, monitoring solutions should be in place that check the application and the infrastructure in which the application is deployed. Gaining fast feedback about the behavior of the production system will adjust processes accordingly. Without efficient monitoring, automatic

---

[10]See http://www.slideshare.net/jedi4ever/using-monitoring-and-metrics-to-learn-in-development.

releasing can result in shots in the dark, where you release continuously without knowing (in the sense of qualifying and measuring) the result.

Tools like Nagios, Collectd, Ganglia, or Munin should be your daily companion to gain insight about the state of your production system. Services like Pingdom, New Relic, or Datadog even provide "monitoring as a service," which means Cloud-based monitoring solutions.[11]

Now that I've introduced aspects of automatic releasing, let's look into more details about how you can perform automatic releasing, incrementally and iteratively, by decoupling deployment and release.

Decoupled Deployment and Release

Let's look at some key mechanics on how to decouple deployment and release, which can be of big help for implementing DevOps. Decoupling deployment and release improves and accelerates delivery, which is one building block of DevOps.

Branch by Abstraction

Branch by abstraction incrementally makes large-scale changes to your system. The strategy to branch by abstraction was initially introduced by Paul Hammant.[12] In his blog post,[13] Jez Humble detailed the strategy and provides a concrete use case. According to Jez Humble the main steps for implementing the strategy include:

1. Create an abstraction over the part of the system that you need to change.

2. Refactor the rest of the system to use the abstraction layer.

3. Continue coding; the abstraction layer delegates to the old or new code, as required.

4. Remove the old implementation.

5. Iterate over steps 3 and 4. Ship your system in the meantime.

6. Once the old implementation has been completely replaced, remove the abstraction layer.

Feature Toggles

The concept of a feature toggle is to deliver the complete code to production but use data-driven switches to decide which feature is made available during runtime. To enable data-driven switches, configuration files are often used. With feature toggles, the team can develop on the

---

[11] http://www.nagios.org; http://collectd.org; http://ganglia.info; http://munin-monitoring.org; http://www.pingdom.co; http://newrelic.co; http://www.datadoghq.com.
[12] See http://paulhammant.com/blog/branch_by_abstraction.html.
[13] See http://continuousdelivery.com/2011/05/make-large-scale-changes-incrementally-with-branch-by-abstraction/.

same development mainline (without the need for using branches) and ship the complete code to production.

To illustrate this strategy, Martin Fowler introduces the example of a web application where you use Java server page (JSP) tags to surround any user interface parts of a feature that should not be made available.[14]

Feature toggles can help to degrade your service gracefully under load. This ability to restore your system to a baseline state is vital not just when a deployment goes wrong but also as part of your disaster recovery strategy. One of the concepts introduced by ITIL is remediation, defined as "recovery to a known state after a failed change or release."[15]

■ **Note**   ITIL, the Information Technology Infrastructure Library, is a set of practices for IT service management that focuses on aligning IT services with the needs of a business.

The advantage of feature toggles is a disadvantage too: although fading out features in production, the production code does contain parts that are not relevant for that specific release. This nonrelevant code may influence other code parts or even provoke errors. Additionally, fading out features on the user interface may easily be possible, but it may not be possible to fade out corresponding functionality in the backend of the application.

Dark Launching

Dark launching is the strategy of deploying first versions of functionality into production before releasing the functionality to all users. The term *dark launching* was coined by the creators of Facebook.[16] Dark launching decouples the deployment of a new version of software from the release of the features within it. You can deploy new versions of the software continuously, regardless of which features are available to which users.

With first versions in production made available for a subset of end users only, you can find any bugs more easily, before you make the release available to all users.

Dark launching provides an approach to remediate in a low-risk way. If problems occur with an early version of a feature, only a few users may experience the problem. Additionally, you can address the incident without a complete heavyweight rollback, just by switching off the feature (e.g., by a feature toggle) or by changing a router setting. Dark launching can be combined with blue-green deployments, which we'll discover next.

Blue-Green Deployment

Another pattern for releasing software iteratively and incrementally is the blue-green deployment. The core of this strategy is that we deploy the new version of the application side by side

---

[14]See http://martinfowler.com/bliki/FeatureToggle.html.
[15]See the glossary under: http://www.itil-officialsite.com/InternationalActivities/ITILGlossaries_2.aspx.
[16]See http://www.facebook.com/note.php?note_id=14218138919.

with the old version. To switch over to the new version or roll back to the old version, back and forth, we merely have to change a load balancer or router setting.

Blue-green deployment ensures that you have two production environments that are as similar as possible. At any one time, one of them (e.g., the green environment) is live. While bringing a new release of your software to production, you conduct the final steps of testing in the blue environment. Once the software is working in the blue environment as expected, configurations are done, and smoke tests are run successfully, we switch the router to redirect all incoming requests to go to the blue environment. Afterward, the green environment is out of production and can be used to prepare the next release.

A variation on blue-green deployment that can be applied when running a cluster of servers is "canary releasing". Here, rather than upgrading a whole cluster to the latest version all at once, you deploy incrementally. The new release first goes to a subset of production systems, to which only specific users or a closed user group (e.g., employees) are routed. If this deployment is successful, the release can be deployed to more users, or finally to all available users. Blue-green deployment, feature toggles, and canary releasing are methods that are often combined with A/B testing. With A/B testing, two versions of software are compared. To determine which version is better, experimentation with both versions are done simultaneously, slightly diversifying one version or the other.

Conclusion

In this chapter, we discussed classic and Agile approaches to measurement and metrics. We discussed how using the change as a key metric can foster a shared understanding between development and operations. A change is a common term that can be applied to all changes in the software, middleware, and infrastructure.

Working with changes directly leads to both the cycle time and batch sizes. Reducing both cycle time and batch sizes is essential for delivering functionality quickly and with low risk.

Automation is a key part of DevOps. Automation is used to gain fast feedback. There are different approaches to optimizing delivery, but pitfalls must also be considered when striving for a high degree of automation.

Part I of this book comes to a close with the end of this chapter. You've learned about the fundamentals of DevOps, which we'll describe in further detail in the remaining parts of this book.

Metrics and Measurement View

This part digs deeper into approaches to share and align goals and incentives. Quality and testing are crucial aspects of DevOps, and we'll cover both of those, as well as team work, here.

Quality and Testing

Is all fun and game until you are need of put it in production.

—DevOps Borat[1]

Everyone discusses quality and wants to improve it. However, not defining quality has the wonderful effect of allowing quality to be everything, including perks such as full pots of coffee on each table. Many projects have experienced excellent results by using tests as a vehicle for measuring quality. This chapter will discuss quality and tests and show their essential relevance for DevOps.

What Is Quality?

The definition of quality is unique to a given context. Gerald M. Weinberg states that "quality is conforming to someone's requirements."[2] Normally, the sponsor of the delivered product (the customer) pays the team to provide the software. In fact, the customer has the right to provide his or her personal definition of quality and determine what he or she wants to spend money on. However, what actually is quality? To bring quality to life, this chapter will introduce some possible attributes of quality. Let's summarize what attributes people think quality can have by starting with the most obvious and traditional ones. Quality may have the following characteristics:

- Expansive test coverage of unit tests; the more coverage, the better.

- A small number of entries in the bug tracker.

- A small number of entries in the bug tracker given a specific priority ranking of entries.

---

[1]http://twitter.com/devops_borat/status/192271992253190144.
[2]*Quality Software Management*, vol. 1 (Dorset House, 1992), p. 5.

- Minimization of accidental complexity, which is complexity that is not inherent to the task to be solved (whereas inherent complexity is essential for solving the specific task).

- Compliance with defined metrics that are measured with Checkstyle,[3] PMD,[4] or FindBugs.[5]

- Compliance with system runtime quality, including functionality, performance, security, availability, resilience, usability, and interoperability.

- Compliance with system non-runtime quality, including modifiability, portability, reusability, and testability.

- Excellent stability and capacity of the software.

- Free coffee for the whole team at any time.

Additionally, there are more subtle quality attributes, such as the following:

- A good business quality, including costs, schedule, marketability, and appropriateness for the organization.

- A good overall cycle time, as discussed in Chapter 3.

DEFINITIONS: CAPACITY AND RESILIENCE

The maximum throughput a system can sustain for a given workload while maintaining an acceptable response time for each individual transaction is its capacity (Michael T. Nygard, *Release It!* The Pragmatic Programmers, 2007, p. 152).

Resilience is the intrinsic ability of a system to adjust its functioning prior to, during, or following changes and disturbances, so that it can sustain required operations under both expected and unexpected conditions.(Hollnagel et.al, *Resilience Engineering in Practice*, Ashgate Publishing, 2011, page xxxvi)

As shown by these few examples, quality can mean many different things. Let's now group quality attributes into leading and supporting attributes.

Leading and Supporting Attributes

Interestingly, people who claim that all aspects of quality are important—such as good test coverage or the stability of the application—are correct. However, the first examples in the list I just provided are supporting attributes, and the final ones, which I labeled in a slightly provocative way as "subtle," are leading (i.e., necessary) attributes, namely business quality and cycle time.

---

[3]http://checkstyle.sourceforge.net.
[4]http://pmd.sourceforge.net.
[5]http://findbugs.sourceforge.net.

Supporting attributes can be helpful in specific contexts as well, although attributes such as "number of entries in the bug tracker" are not meaningful and can be manipulated easily, as discussed in Chapter 3. For the DevOps approach, we are more interested in comprehensive, objective, measureable values that are meaningful for both development and operations. Development and operations can integrate and align themselves with these leading quality attributes. These attributes are vehicles for better cooperation and shared goals.

Measurable Attributes

One point is obviously true for all possible quality attributes: to know whether a specific quality has been achieved (or not achieved), it has to be measured. As soon as you have a measured value, you can benchmark it and try to improve it.

Supporters of "systems thinking" theories will protest because they argue that systems consist of numerous interdependencies, which create the need to deal with chaos and complexity. In scenarios of chaos theory, multiloop, nonlinear feedback systems produce chaotic behavior.[6] However, giving up the struggle to continuously improve and dealing explicitly with quality is the first step of chaos. What we also see in DevOps is that quality attributes influence one another. For example, if the application is not stable, its costs and marketability may be affected as well.

Reliability on Context

In addition to the interdependencies of quality attributes, quality heavily relies on context. Let me give one example: the stability of the application is based on various factors, such as what users do with the application and how many users perform this function. Decisions directly impact qualities, and a decision in favor of one quality often impacts another. Quality must be set in context, and often, the best solution is a compromise and a matter of prioritizing the different quality attributes. Dedicated teams (such as development and operations) may have other priorities for quality attributes or may not want to deal with attributes from other groups. Thus, to obtain the best overall solution, teams must define quality in a holistic way, spanning all project roles and phases. Leading attributes are the best candidates for a well-rounded definition of quality because they feature a holistic macrofocus rather than a microfocus.

Once again, I don't intend to make any supporting attributes look small. Their supportive character can deliver important insights about the software. The software must obey their respective target values for quality as a necessary condition, but matching these values is not a sufficient condition. Let me give you two examples:

- Although Checkstyle, PMD, FindBugs, and Sonar (that are running as part of your continuous build) detect design and code flaws, the code may not be a good release candidate (perhaps because it does not implement all functional requirements). However, if the audits in your continuous build detect any design and code flaws, the application is not a release candidate.

---

[6]For more details, consult Jamshid Gharajedaghi, *Systems Thinking: Managing Chaos and Complexity* (Morgan Kaufmann, 2011).

- Although the application passed all tests, it may not be a good release candidate (perhaps because other quality attributes haven't met). If a single test fails, the application is not a release candidate.

▓ **Note**   Sonar (`http://www.sonarsource.org/`) is a tool for continuous inspection. It can inspect applications that are written in many different languages including Java, Cobol, PHP, and C++. For Java, Sonar does integrate with tools that inspect the quality of Java applications, including Checkstyle (`http://checkstyle.sourceforge.net/`), PMD (`http://pmd.sourceforge.net`), and FindBugs (`http://findbugs.sourceforge.net/`). There are many tools for checking infrastructure as well. For style checking on infrastructure (checking if Puppet manifests confirm to the style guide), puppet-lint could be used, see `https://github.com/rodjek/puppet-lint`.

Key Aspects of Quality

Let's now summarize the key findings about quality. In defining quality, the following tasks must be performed:

- Define what quality is in your context.
- Describe quality in terms of scenarios that put quality into context.
- Distinguish between supportive and leading quality attributes.
- Appreciate the dependencies among attributes.
- Emphasize the attributes that are crucial for success.
- Build quality into your process, spanning all activities of software engineering, including development and operations.

Ultimately, quality comes down to the behavior of the software in production and the cycle time.

▓ **Note**   Don't forget: Injecting quality into your application, ex post, will not work!

Although subjective valuations of quality can be useful, objective measurements of quality should be preferred. Therefore, distinguish between the necessary and sufficient conditions for quality and acknowledge quality as a holistic goal that must be shared across teams.

Now that we know what quality is, we can now discuss how to improve quality.

Patterns for Improving Quality

To define quality is a very good start. But we want to improve quality continuously. In this section I'll show you some patterns for improving quality.

Let's list some patterns for improving quality across all teams. We'll start by distinguishing between internal and external quality.

Internal and External Quality

To understand and measure quality, we must distinguish between internal and external quality. *Internal quality* is the quality of the design and code.[7] Internal quality can be improved by applying good design[8] and coding[9] practices and a sustainable development and delivery process. *External quality* is measured by what you see while using the application. Even if the external quality is great (all functions are available), the internal quality may be very bad (bad code and code that is not maintainable). In the case of poor internal quality, the external quality will also suffer eventually because the application will raise an increasing number of bugs. Additionally, development time will increase because of the increased technical debt.

Use Scenarios to Describe Quality

One good approach for building quality into the process is to describe quality attributes in terms of scenarios such as the following: If ten users initiate logout actions, the logout component will process the requests with an average latency of one second under normal circumstances. This scenario allows the team to make quantifiable arguments about a system. In DevOps, it is important to identify connections and see implications for the whole system. Scenarios are useful for managing a given complex structure with its connections to other structures. For example, if a developer changes a core part of the client–server connection of an application, this must be tested thoroughly on target systems, not only by the developer but also by operations. Although the development desktop may (hopefully) be similar to the production system in many parts, it will not be exactly the same, especially not in areas of processes and threads that are essentially influenced by changes in the client–server connection. A scenario description consists of a source of stimulus (e.g., users), the actual stimulus (e.g., initiated transaction), the artifact affected (e.g., logout component), the environment in which it exists (e.g., normal operation), the effect of the action (e.g., transaction processed), and the response measure (e.g., within one second). Writing such detailed statements is only possible if the relevant requirements have been identified and an idea of the components has been proposed. A more detailed example of a scenario for availability of an application is shown in Table 4–1.[10]

Now that we understand quality scenarios, let's discover how quality is an inherent part.

Table 4–1. *Availability Scenario*

Scenario Item	Possible Values
Source	Internal to the system; external to the system
Stimulus	Fault: omission, crash, timing, response
Artifact	System's processors, communication channels, persistent storage, processes

(continued)

---

[7]Reminder: if we talk about "code," we mean all types of code that make up the solution, including application code, infrastructure code, and automation scripting.
[8]See Erich Gamma et al., *Design Patterns* (Addison-Wesley, 1994).
[9]See Robert C. Martin, *Clean Code* (Prentice Hall, 2008).
[10]See Len Bass, Paul Clements, and Rick Kazman, *Software Architecture in Practice* (Addison-Wesley, 2003), p. 81.

Table 4–1. (*Continued*)

Scenario Item	Possible Values
Environment	Normal operation; degraded mode (i.e., fewer features, a fallback solution)
Response	System should detect event and do one or more of the following: record it; notify appropriate parties, including the user and other systems; disable sources of events that cause fault or failure according to defined rules; be unavailable for a prespecified interval, where interval depends on criticality of system; continue to operate in normal or degraded mode
Response measure	Time interval when the system must be available; available time; time interval in which system can be in degraded mode; repair time

Quality Is an Inherent Part

Quality in software engineering is important at all times, from the very beginning until the application is running and is maintained in production. Quality can't be injected into the application post mortem. For example, if an application isn't designed and developed for high performance, it can hardly be run as a high-performance application in production. Additionally, it's not sufficient to improve on a local scope, or to expect any great quality improvements by micro-tuning individual software units. As W. Edwards Deming states in his book *Out of Crisis* (MIT Press, 2010), "Any substantial improvement must come from action on the system" (page 7) and "Quality comes not from inspection, but from improvement of the production process" (page 29). Deming raised fourteen points to improve in a holistic way (page 23), including to build quality into the product in the first place, improve constantly and forever the system of production and service, to institute training on the job, to drive out fear, to eliminate management by objective and to break down barriers between departments.

QA and Making Quality Visible

QA is performed by the whole team, including development and operations. You can ensure the quality of an application only if you have control over that application. If you don't have the authority to change the application, you can't ensure its quality. Of course you can evaluate it and report the result to someone else. But real and holistic QA can only be done if you can change the solution (with its parts application, middleware, and infrastructure), thus, bringing together development and operations.

With DevOps, quality is an inherent part of the approach. Instead of being an explicit downstream activity, QA is done at any time and by the whole team (especially by development and operations). In our previous example of the high-performance application, DevOps suggests that development and operations are working closely to develop the high-performance application and bring it to production together.

Quality is made visible by applying "continuous integration"[11] (that is, in short, a shared agreement in the team that when the team gets the latest code from the code repository, it will

---

[11] See Paul M. Duvall et al., *Continuous Integration* (Addison-Wesley, 2007).

always build successfully and pass all tests, with the prerequisite that the team checks in their code every few hours[12]) and "continuous delivery"[13] (that is, in short, continuously stage software through a delivery pipeline, from development to production). A crucial observation is that quality gains further momentum the closer we get to production (operations). The main reason for this is that it is often not the software you bring to production that you *wish* to bring to production. What you bring to production is the *real* software with its actual quality. There might be a big difference between the wish and the reality, or in other words, between the result of concepts and versions of the software in development and the result of the same software running on real production machines. Deployment and running in production closes the *definition of done*. Having the software in production is the moment when you see that you've done your work accurately. There is no replacement for software running in production from both perspectives, gaining business value and gaining meaningful (technical) insight about the quality.

Degeneration: Faults and Failures

Over time, if you don't pay attention to the quality of software, software can degenerate. Degeneration happens, for example, if too many versions are pushed to production, with the application having suboptimal internal quality, and many more upcoming requirements should be implemented in the software. Other worse-case scenarios include automation that is not tested and packing and deploying the software to production when it is error-prone; monitoring is not in place; or nonfunctional requirements were not implemented accordingly (e.g., because the operations team was not consulted early enough). High-speed releasing, together with a high portion of technical debt, leads to degeneration, which has consequences. In particular, degeneration of quality at the beginning of the process negatively affects the entire process, with self-reinforcing results (i.e. degeneration of quality will probably lead to more degeneration of quality) . Hence, you must take care of all quality attributes from the very beginning of the process. This point may be obvious, but many teams fail to adhere to this principle. It will not work to inject quality into the software post mortem.

Taking quality as an inherent part will reduce both the amount and the impact of faults. According to Weinberg, "A fault is the defect in the program that, when executed under particular conditions, causes a failure." He further defines failure as "the departure of the external results of program operation from requirement."[14] Obviously, inherent quality will decrease the amount of faults by identifying, isolating, and addressing defects early and keeping the internal quality up. But what is also reduced by the DevOps approach is the impact of faults, meaning the failures. This is achieved by aligning your work with the "building blocks" of DevOps, which were introduced in Chapter 3.

Because quality attributes must be taken care of from the start, you have to address the challenge of dealing with quality that is traditionally detected or important for project roles in the later steps of the delivery chain. For example, although the stability of an application may be crucial for operations, that stability must be built into the application during the prior development phase. Quality attributes must be an inherent part of the software development

---

[12]See Rachel Davies, Liz Sedley, *Agile Coaching* (The Pragmatic Bookshelf, 2009).
[13]See Jez Humble, David Farley, *Continuous Delivery* (Addison-Wesley, 2011).
[14]*Quality Software Management*, vol. 2 (Dorset House, 1993), p. 237.

and delivery process from the beginning. Quality attributes can be implemented at the start by aligning work not with artifacts but with project roles. Development and operations have distinct views of the world and the project roles around them. Each department will do the right thing, but their self-interests may not correspond to the best interest for the whole company.

Test Automation Mix

In a software delivery process, you should detect flaws and bugs as soon as possible. Automated tests provide fast and continuous feedback on the state and quality of the software. Automated tests provide a safety net required to add new features and incorporate bug fixes without breaking existing features. The whole team is responsible for test automation (including development and operations).

It is important to understand that, although it is crucial to use automated tests, not all tests can be automated, e.g. usability tests, exploratory tests or one-off tests[15].

The test automation mix includes unit tests, service tests and UI tests, see the test automation pyramid[16] (Figure 4-1). Although you should use all three categories of tests, the basis of your test strategy should be formed by unit tests, that we'll explore next.

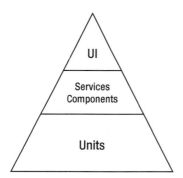

Figure 4-1. *The testing pyramid: the fundament is a broad base of unit tests. Tests for services are based on the unit tests. User interface (UI) tests are the top of the pyramid.*

Unit Testing

The base of automatic testing should be thorough unit test coverage.

Unit tests will test single units, often in a class. There are no dependencies on other resources (e.g., databases), other subsystems, or other components (which comprise a collection of classes). The xUnit tool family is the de facto standard for unit testing code. You can run unit tests in developer workspaces and in a central integrative environment on your build server.

---

[15] For more information, see Lisa Crisping and Janet Gregory, *Agile Testing* (Addison-Wesley, 2009), p. 285.
[16] See Mike Cohn, *Succeeding with Agile* (Addison-Wesley, 2010), p. 312.

Integration tests bridge different units and often access databases and other (remote) systems. These service tests run longer than unit tests and should be triggered on the build server only. On top of the pyramid, user interface (UI) tests trigger graphical controls and drive the UI. They can be automated as well by using adequate drivers. Exploratory tests are an example of a UI test that should be performed by a human.

Testing the configuration management is still uncommon, despite its great potential. There are many ways to test a declarative system in operations to verify the system's behavior. One powerful approach to express the behavior of your infrastructure as code is Cucumber-puppet.[17] Cucumber is a framework for applying BDD, and Cucumber-puppet and rspec-puppet[18] allow you to test Puppet manifests.

Practices such as test-driven development recommend writing tests first and writing functional and test code in small iterations along with refactorings to improve the code design.[19] A broad selection of unit tests is essential for fast feedback cycles and to improve the quality of the code, particularly its design. Approaches can simulate ("mock") other components and subsystems during the testing of a unit.

Service Tests

The layer of services and components comprises different units. These integration tests connect multiple components and test the system as a whole without touching the UI. White box tests are similar to unit tests and service or component tests. That is, they test how a specific test was passed. One powerful tool that drives integration tests is Arquillian. The mission of Arquillian is to provide a test harness that decouples the test logic from the container lifecycle and deployment specifics such that the team can easily set up integration tests.[20] Those tests are abstracted from the environment where they run. Because Arquillian can either execute a test case inside the container or hold back the test class, it can act as a remote client to the deployed code.

UI Testing

UI testing inherently tests the application, the middleware and the infrastructure. UI testing is also important, but it comprises only a small part of the overall testing strategies. UI tests are black box tests: they answer certain questions (e.g., "What is a specific task?") and thus test whether the application executes its defined behavior. UIs and their controls, order of controls, and layout may change dramatically over time. Additionally, UI tests must be maintained in a manner similar to how business code must be maintained. To reduce effort and minimize false positives, tests should be simple and robust. Because UI tests are brittle, expensive to write, and time consuming, you should decouple your tests from the UI. For example, don't test if clicking a submit button actually creates a new entry in the database. Rather, introduce a thorough unit test base and set the service tests (i.e., those services that are called by clicking the button on the UI) on top. In your UI tests, you should decouple the UI tests from the context.

---

[17] https://github.com/nistude/cucumber-puppet.
[18] https://github.com/rodjek/rspec-puppet
[19] For details, see Kent Beck, *Test-Driven Development* (Addison-Wesley, 2003).
[20] http://www.jboss.org/arquillian.

For example, to identify the controls on the UI, you should use relative paths with, for example, XPath expressions or HTML's "name" attribute.

Find the test coverage for UI tests with a great value-to-effort ratio. For example, it may be sufficient to set up smoke tests that are run automatically after a new release of the application is rolled out to a target environment. As discussed in Chapter 3, smoke tests give the application a quick shot that starts checking whether the application is available and whether the users can navigate through the happy paths (main scenarios). Instead of testing all use cases on the UI, you may only wish to test a relevant subset of important use cases. However, you can test all use cases on the UI, and doing so may be the best solution for a given context.

UI tests often connect external subsystems and include network services, databases, file system access, and so on. Thus, UI tests test the most important thing: how the application works. James Whittaker, Jason Arbon, and Jeff Carollo distinguish between different test sizes and introduce small, medium and large tests[21]. UI tests are large tests that have a broad scope (meaning when a test fails, the cause might be difficult to find). Large tests often make it difficult and time-consuming to setup test data.

One powerful example of using web UI tests is the use of Selenium 2 (WebDriver).[22] Selenium has different running modes where you can choose between driving a real Internet browser to test your application and simulating a browser. The former validates the behavior of the application under real conditions, whereas the latter allows UI tests to be run with fast feedback cycles. UI tests are often considered to be end-user acceptance tests. Good acceptance should be data driven and written in a ubiquitous language in the form of executable specifications. This approach is often called "specification by example," which we'll discuss in Chapter 10.

Errors in Test Strategy

A common error in test strategy is to not start testing with the fundament of the pyramid. For example, a common antipattern skips unit tests and even service tests and only sets up and runs UI tests[23]. The idea to use UI tests for testing the software with all its parts (application, middleware, infrastructure) is charming. But consider the disadvantages too. As a result of overemphasizing automatic UI tests, the following problems emerge:

- Gaining feedback takes too much time, especially for bug fixes.

- Isolating bugs becomes more difficult.

- The inner quality of the whole application will suffer because units are not covered by tests.

- The design suffers because tests help to improve the design of the software.

---

[21] See *How Google Tests Software* (Addison-Wesley, 2012), page 46.
[22] http://seleniumhq.org.
[23] Some projects even don't run UI tests. If you don't run either unit, or service, or UI tests as part of your automatic build process, then you have a serious problem.

■ **Note** Sometimes it is appropriate to distinguish between testing and checking. Michael Bolton has limited the scope of checking to observations and decisions rules that can be executed without sapience—without a brain-engaged human. If something requires human sapience, it is testing, not checking (see `http://www.developsense.com/2009/09/elements-of-testing-and-checking.html`).

Another common error is to scope tests to application code. One advantage of UI tests is that they use the code across all architectural layers and boundaries, such as application, middleware, and infrastructure. But how should you proceed with unit tests and service tests? Don't solely apply them to the application itself. Instead, unit test infrastructure (e.g., by rspec-puppet) or infrastructure services by evolving monitoring.

Acceptance Criteria

When using an Agile process framework like Scrum,[24] it is important to include good acceptance criteria to your product backlog items. Acceptance criteria define what needs to be fulfilled so that the story may be marked as complete. Good acceptance criteria define when you're done ("definition of done"). According to Ken Schwaber and Jeff Sutherland, "The backlog is an ordered list of everything that might be needed in the product and is the single source of requirements for any changes to be made to the product."[25] For general advice on how to deal with backlogs, see chapter 29 of Mitch Lacey's *The Scrum Field Guide* (Addison-Wesley, 2012). More on acceptance tests will be discussed in Chapter 10.

Test aspects are crucial parts of your backlog. You should always try to ensure testable stories by defining a test case. You should also estimate testing efforts when estimating a user story for your backlog.

Inject Quality Gates

There are many ways to check if quality is accurate. With Scrum, strategies include the definition of and alignment with the definition of done, or the demonstration of the iteration result after the iteration is completed. Although QA should be done by the whole team at any time in development, having quality gates can be of value. A quality gate is a milestone during delivery where special quality requirements are checked. If the requirements are fulfilled, the software may be staged further into the direction of production until it is in production and available for the users. Optimally, quality gates can fail automatically to maximize the flow and minimize cumbersome, manual activities. However, there are different contexts. Some projects obtain good results by not introducing quality gates. These results suggest that any type of quality gate is a potential bottleneck that prevents features from being delivered to the customer.

---

[24] Scrum is an abstract management framework, the free Scrum primer can be download at `http://scrumfoundation.com/library`.
[25] See their *Software in 30 Days* (Wiley, 2012), p. 129.

Typical use cases for quality gates include the following:

- The continuous build fails if the checked-in code provokes test failures.

- The continuous build fails if the test coverage of new code fails to meet the coverage goals.

- The continuous build fails if Checkstyle, PMD, or FindBugs detects a design or code flow with severe "errors."

- The automatic QA build fails if Sonar throws an "Alert."

- The QA build fails if the automatic acceptance tests fail.

- The release build fails if the application still depends on components that in turn are still under development (and thus not released yet in a specific version).

- Rollout to production fails if the BDD tests fail to check the behavior of the infrastructure.

- Any further rollout is stopped if check-ins to the infrastructure code provoke build errors.

- Software development stops if project's coffee depot is used up.

Let's now take a deeper look at a concrete example of a quality gate.

Example of a Quality Gate

Let's now examine more closely what a quality gate might look like. Consider the following infrastructure of open-source tools. We have the following:

- A build that is based on Maven.[26]

- A continuous integration infrastructure that is based on Jenkins.

- A continuous inspection tool named Sonar. In Sonar, we configured the build-breaker plug-in[27] and a profile that verifies coding rules. One coding rule checks for "empty catch blocks" by defining such a bug as one with a "critical" severity. In Sonar, we also configured an "alert" that is activated if the number of critical violations is greater than 0. If an alert is raised, the underlying build will fail.

---

[26]These are examples. You can also develop an effective solution by integrating Gradle, Hudson, and Sonar.

[27]Documentation about the plug-in can be found at http://docs.codehaus.org/display/SONAR/Build+Breaker.

▓ **Note**   Jenkins (http://jenkins-ci.org/) is a continuous integration server that can build and deploy your applications. For Java, many build tools exist that can compile, test, package, and deploy your applications, including Maven (http://maven.apache.org/), Gradle (http://www.gradle.org/), and Ant (http://ant.apache.org/).

In the workspace, the code that was developed has an empty catch block (see Listing 4-1).

Listing 4-1. *A Java try clause with an empty catch block.*

```
try {
if (integer1 == integer2) {
        System.out.println("..");
    }
} catch (Throwable t) {}
```

After the code is checked into version control, such as Subversion or Git, our continuous integration engine (Jenkins) detects the change and starts the continuous build (we'll explore strategies and tool chains in more detail in Chapter 8 when we discuss automatic releasing). After compiling and unit testing the classes, the code is validated with Sonar.

▓ **Note**   Subversion (http://subversion.apache.org/) and Git (http://git-scm.com/) are version control systems. For more information, please consult the respective documentation.

Sonar detects whether a quality gate (defined as an "alert") failed. As a result, because of the empty catch block, Sonar fails the Jenkins build. Listing 4-2 shows the relevant example error code in the Jenkins console log.

Listing 4-2. *A Java try clause with an empty catch block.*

```
[ERROR] Critical violations > 0
[INFO] ------------------------------------------------------------------------
[INFO] Reactor Summary:
[INFO]
[INFO] RocketScience ...................................... FAILURE [45.599s]
[INFO] moduleA ............................................ SUCCESS [3.650s]
[INFO] moduleB ............................................ SUCCESS [2.714s]
[INFO] ------------------------------------------------------------------------
[INFO] BUILD FAILURE
[INFO] ------------------------------------------------------------------------
[INFO] Total time: 46.285s
[INFO] Finished at: Sun Jan 01 16:04:45 CET 2012
[INFO] Final Memory: 14M/44M
[INFO] ------------------------------------------------------------------------
```

```
[ERROR] Failed to execute goal org.codehaus.mojo:sonar-maven-plugin:2.0:sonar
(default-cli) on project multi-module: Cannot execute Sonar: Alert thresholds
have been hit (1 times). ->[Help 1]
```

Navigating to the Sonar web UI, we'll examine in greater detail the number of violations and failed quality gates. In our example, the number of critical alerts is 1, as shown in Figure 4–2.

Figure 4–2. *Sonar dashboard showing different metrics, including "alerts." We've configured the system to fail the build if the number of critical violations is greater than 0.*

As you can see, a tool chain of Maven, Jenkins, and Sonar is flexible enough to set up powerful quality gates. If the defined quality gates aren't met, the build server Jenkins can fail the build. If the quality gate is passed, further down-streamed jobs can be triggered on the way to promote the software until it is in production. These uses of quality gates are not limited to functional code written, for example, in Java, rather quality gates can be used for infrastructure as code and acceptance tests too. You can also set up your build server to listen to changes in your infrastructure (see Chapter 9) or your specifications (see Chapter 10). Thus, this approach is an advanced strategy designed to bridge development with operations.

Conclusion

In this chapter, we discussed quality. We distinguished between the leading and supportive attributes of quality. All attributes can be helpful and important, but the customer ultimately determines his or her priorities and for which attributes he or she wants to pay money.[28] DevOps prefers holistic, leading quality attributes, especially the cycle time. You learned about different strategies for measuring and improving quality. Quality should be an inherent part of the process. You should always consider the test automation mix and quality gates.

---

[28]Quality costs money. Having bad quality costs even more money.

Introduce Shared Incentives

In startup we are use new technique call 5 Why not Me for show how nobody is of blame for outage.

—DevOps Borat[1]

This chapter will discuss shared incentives. You'll learn how to evolve a team from a working group and you'll discover that goals, working agreements, and motivation are essential for creating shared incentives. I'll introduce patterns to become a team. Finally, we go through two real-world success stories, which illustrate how to bring all of these different aspects together. But let's start with the war story of the magic kingdoms.

War Study: Magic Kingdoms

I once helped out on a project that delivered its software to an operations team. The development and operations teams were located on different floors of the building. There was some magic atmosphere between them, and I soon understood why.

The company set up a thorough process to hand over software to operations: The development team had to fill in some forms to describe what the software was about, its architecture, and important aspects. Almost no tests were written, neither functional acceptance tests nor unit tests. The development was not a balance of skills and experience: many programmers were rookies (who were not coached by the seniors) and a few were seniors. At the beginning, no testing activities were involved except that done by the programmers themselves.

Handover of software and documents to operations was pretty chaotic: it was not always clear which version of code and documents was the final release version. It was no surprise that the quality of the software was very bad. But the bad quality did not became visible before it reached production. This caused problems for the operations team, which had to bring the software into production, because the rollout process was always broken. The rollout onto the production systems was more a trial-and-error than a prescribed process of configuring the software for target environments.

---

[1] http://twitter.com/devops_borat/status/210810075240083457.

Management was confronted with decreasing team morale, finger pointing at the dedicated departments, poor quality software, as well as a long rollout process. Consequently, management decided to introduce even more forms to be filled out before transitioning the software into operations. Finally, the management thought it found a good new approach when it introduced management by objectives (MBOs), where development had the objective of delivering high-quality software and operations focused on the objective to promote the software to production once it had no bugs.

What was the result? As a consequence of the new MBOs, no new software was put into production at all. The operations team got its full bonus through ensuring stability by refusing to roll out changes to production. Although the development team improved, its software was not accepted by operations. This escalated the situation between the departments. Escalation meetings led to even more finger pointing, to the point where people were calling one another liars. This arose because what was said in escalation meetings was not always the same as what people said in face-to-face conversations between engineers.

Middle management introduced writing more paperware by writing meeting minutes that clearly addressed action items and responsibilities. Middle management also prohibited communication among the teams except during the time when meetings occurred. The bottom line is that the management did everything to foster two magic kingdoms. Each team believed it did everything right and that its decisions and behavior were aligned with the team's goals.

After this war story, let's now explore how to do better, and start with discussing what a team is.

What Is a Team?

A team is a working group in which members work together closely, cooperatively, and interdependently to achieve a shared group goal.[2] Besides the goal, the team has agreed on an approach to the work (e.g., by sharing the "definition of done") and a consensus culture at work. Often the team has complementary skills. This means that every role has equal value (e.g., colleagues from development and operations), and the sum of all roles forms the team in which anyone can pick up tasks. Teams are not too big (e.g., teams may have up to ten members at most). The optimal size of a team depends on the complexity of the task to be accomplished. Too many members complicates team building and increases misunderstandings and the amount of communication pairs.

▓ **Note**   Everything affects the behavior of the team and its members: chairs, seating, shape of the building, and whether people share a native language. Walls act as barriers, and open space acts as a conduit.

As Alistair Cockburn states, teams form communities and are ecosystems.[3] Although having personal goals and personal knowledge, on teams, people pull approximately in the same direction.

---

[2] See Gerald M. Weinberg, *The Psychology of Computer Programming* (Dorset House, 1998), "Establishing and Accepting Goals" page 72.
[3] See Alistair Cockburn, *Agile Software Development: The Cooperative Game* (Addison-Wesley, 2007), chap. 3.

In order to become a team, it is essential for the group to share goals and commit to working agreements, which we'll discuss next.

Goals and Working Agreements

"When people have a common goal, make commitments to each other about their interdependent tasks, and use an agreed-upon approach to the work, they are part of a team. If you want your team to jell, help them determine some short-term goals that they can accomplish only together."[4] A goal is a desired result the team plans and commits to achieve. Every team member has individual goals that must be aligned with the overall goal of the whole team. "Goals have to be real and easily recognizable as valuable."[5] For team building, the concrete goal may be less important. As Tom DeMarco states "Getting the system built was an arbitrary goal, but the team had accepted it. It was what they had formed around. From the time of jelling, the team itself had been the real focus for their energies. They were in it for joint success, the pleasure of achieving the goal, and any goal, together."[6]

It can be helpful for the team to start by determining what is its real commitment to quality, and then make that commitment meaningful, not letting obstacles discourage them. To build quality into the developed product, and thus also into the development and delivery process, is an often used approach in great teams. "The best professionals and craftspersons alike aspire to build quality products; it is a point of pride."[7]

Setting up concepts, particularly requirements documents, is essential for fostering agreement (see Chapter 6).

Working agreements guide the daily work of the team. According to Diana Larsen and Ainsley Nies, the following aspects are important for Agile chartering and to foster collaboration[8]:

- An explicit set of agreements about how a team functions provides clarity that prevents confusion and conflict later.

- Teams function together in many ways, and every team does it somewhat differently. You can only assume that everyone shares the same understandings if you have discussed and documented them.

- Working agreements help new members learn how to participate constructively. They serve as the basic list of key dos and don'ts.

- In meetings, explicit working agreements help members stay accountable, because if they violate an agreement, any other member can point out what they agreed to.

---

[4] Johanna Rothman, *Manage It!* (Pragmatic Bookshelf, 2007), page 123.
[5] Johanna Rothman and Esther Derby, *Behind Closed Doors* (Pragmatic Bookshelf, 2005), page 49.
[6] Tom DeMarco and Timothy Lister, *Peopleware*, 2nd ed. (Dorset House, 1999), page 125.
[7] Eric Ries, *The Lean Startup* (Portfolio Penguin, 2011), page 106.
[8] Diana Larsen and Ainsley Nies, *Liftoff: Launching Agile Teams & Projects* (Onyx Neon Press, 2012), chap. 8.

THE HAWTHORNE EFFECT

Between 1924 and 1932 a series of experiments were done in a factory called Hawthorne Works that led to the term *Hawthorne effect.*[9] In psychology, the effect describes the fact that persons change their behavior when they know they are members of a research or study. Thus it's possible that the result of research is directly influenced by the research itself. Transported to DevOps, by introducing DevOps to your company and initially discussing goals and working agreements, you may already experience significant improvements.

Examples of team-related working agreements include:

- *Moving forward*: Any member may ask for a test for agreement at any time. Others may clarify the question that was raised, and all indicate their level of agreement.

- *Wise use of meeting time*: Stick to one conversation at a time in meetings.

- *Decisions*: Make team decisions according to type. First, decide how you will decide. In some contexts, voting can be a good choice, in others abiding by decisions of the most qualified team members. In some cases, the team decides through consensus. In contrast to *command*, *delegation*, or *democratic* decision models, consensus builds support (team members are enthusiastic to be collectively part of the decision process) and reduces risk (robust decisions backed by all members of the team).[10]

- *Feedback*: Seek and offer feedback on the impact of actions and interactions. Also use I messages to express feelings, beliefs, and values.[11]

- *Time*: When team meetings are set, make an effort to attend, be on time, come prepared, help the team stay on task.

- *Learning*: Fail fast, fail often, identify mistakes early. A good approach for learning is to use experiments. The team can try small experiments to find and detail working agreements.

- *Knowledge transfer*: Developers pair with members of operations team and vice versa. Pair only once per day.

- *Collective ownership*: Ask for help when stuck on a task.

---

[9] See http://en.wikipedia.org/wiki/Hawthorne_effect.
[10] For information and examples on consensus decision making, see http://en.wikipedia.org/wiki/Consensus_decision-making.
[11] See http://en.wikipedia.org/wiki/I-message.

Goals and working agreements are essential. The motivation of the whole team is essential too, which we'll discuss next.

Motivation

Motivation is derived from the word *motive*, which means needs or desires. Motivation is the inner driver that pushes toward performing actions. For motivation, it is important to have goals. Achieving those goals is important for further motivation, so it may be a good idea to make those goals manageable and achievable in order to be able to finish what you've started. All those aspects are valid for both individuals and teams. By socializing with others and sharing the same goals, a positive attitude is created, which helps individuals to keep striving toward the goal despite failure and difficulties.

Values are important for motivation too. Jurgen Appelo[12] explains how to motivate people and lists 50 virtues, including respect, trust,[13] openness, focus, courage, commitment, and simplicity.

Work factors that stimulate people's behavior include challenging work, achievement, personal growth, best-of-breed processes and tools, recognition, responsibilities, job satisfaction, team work, success, and creative environments.

Mary and Tom Poppendieck state that the building blocks of motivation are[14]:

- *Belonging*: The team must win or lose as a group.

- *Safety*: No zero defects mentality, rather an atmosphere that tolerates mistakes.

- *Competence*: People want to be involved in something they believe will work. A sentence of competence comes from knowledge and skill, positive feedback, high standards, meeting a difficult challenge, and technical excellence.

- *Progress*: When a team meets an important objective, it's time for a celebration.

In his motivator-hygiene theory, psychologist Frederick Herzberg explained that hygiene factors at work are aspects such as job security, salary, status, working conditions, policies, and fringe benefits. He states "Like hygiene, these factors don't make people healthier or happier. It's their absence that can cause deterioration of health or happiness."[15]

Let's now discuss how we become a team.

---

[12] See Jurgen Appelo, *Management 3.0* (Addison-Wesley, 2011), chap. 5.
[13] See Rachel Davies and Liz Sedley, *Agile Coaching* (Pragmatic Bookshelf, 2009), chap. 2.
[14] Mary Poppendieck and Tom Poppendieck, *Lean Software Development: An Agile Toolkit* (Addison-Wesley, 2003), page 108.
[15] Frederick Herzberg, *One More Time: How Do You Motivate Employees?* (Harvard Business Press, 2008), page 79.

Becoming a Team

It's a process to become a team. In what follows I provide patterns on how to succeed in transforming your work group into a team. You may consider starting with setting up shared definitions as follows:

1. Define foundations: determine shared goals (e.g., in a workshop).

2. Define scope as well as boundaries and context (e.g., what's not in the scope of your definition).

3. Define quick wins, a result that can be achieved quickly and is appreciated by all.

4. Define the path to solution, that is, how you want to come up with shared goals (e.g., with brainstorming).

5. Define next the steps: rearrange and plan next steps to foster shared goals.

6. Define slack time in order to improve your daily work, your team collaboration, and the definitions of shared goals.[16] Slack time enables thinking and analyzing the current working approach.

7. Inspect and iterate.

It's essential to include both development and operations into the process of defining.

Next it's essential to focus on sharing between development and operations. The following items are ideas on how to share together:

*   Celebrate success together (e.g., after a new software release is delivered to the customer).

*   Acknowledge the work of others; development and operations have complementary skills and tasks.

*   Apply shared practices and tools (e.g., continuous integration) across departments.

*   Ask questions and give feedback and interactions, to show interest, to learn, and to foster shared understanding.

*   Emphasize visibility (e.g., with applying Kanban, daily stand-up meetings, or retrospectives).

That's great, but it's not enough. Additionally, you need commitment from both the management and the team. Management should commit to:

*   Allow self-direction (e.g., management must not change cards on the team's Kanban board, see Chapter 6)

---

[16] Gerald M. Weinberg, *Becoming a Technical Leader* (Dorset House, 1986), chap. 23.

- Provide the right motivation (e.g., by removing micromanagement that arises or by telling the team how to accomplish a task, not only what the task is)

- Provide slack time (e.g., time to learn and improve)

- Enable the team to do its job successfully (e.g., by providing and allowing good practices and tools to build up a spirit of excellence)

- Foster training and collaboration by rotating roles (e.g., development and operations) and emphasize general communication strategies (e.g., training how to communicate)

- Accept impacts of physical logistics (e.g., workspaces and sitting arrangements)

If you have shared agreements and commitments in place, then you've set up prerequisites for becoming a team. Let's now discuss what Tuckman's stages of group development contribute to the process of becoming a team.

Tuckman's Stages of Group Development

In 1965 Bruce Tuckman introduced a model for group development.[17] According to the model, the team must go through all four stages to reach a state that enables it to perform. First, the *forming* stage of the team takes place. The individual's behavior is driven by a desire to be accepted by the others, to explore, and to avoid conflict. Groups will then enter the *storming* stage. In this phase, members with different ideas compete for consideration. The team tries to find out how they function independently and together and what leadership model they will accept. Team members open up to one another and confront one another's ideas and perspectives. Some team members will focus on minutiae to evade real issues. This stage is necessary to the growth of the team. The team then enters the *norming* stage if it manages to have one goal and comes to a mutual plan. Some may have to give up their own ideas and agree with others in order to make the team function. In this stage, all team members take the responsibility and have the ambition to work for the success of the team's goals. Some groups never pass this stage and remain in this phase.

Some teams reach the *performing* stage. These high-performing teams are able to function as a unit as the team members find ways to get the job done smoothly and effectively without inappropriate conflict or the need for external supervision. By this time, they are motivated and knowledgeable. The team members are now competent, autonomous, and able to handle the decision-making process without supervision. Dissent is expected and allowed as long as it is channeled through means acceptable to the team.

Any time the team is changed (e.g., new members are added), the group may have to start again with the forming stage. If you enter a team in the storming phase, you may be skeptical about the team's behavior or you may even doubt that this is or will be a team. Always take into account that team building is a process that takes some time and goes through several stages. Facilitators and caretakers can be helpful for team building.

---

[17] See http://en.wikipedia.org/wiki/Tuckman%27s_stages_of_group_development.

Facilitator and Caretakers

Although working groups cannot be forced to act as teams, there are many possible ways to introduce and help the team to form itself. One way is to install a facilitator who helps the team to understand and achieve its goals and assists during the daily work. A special form of a facilitator would be a Scrum master, which is a caretaker who maintains the process and enables the team to do its work. Another form of a caretaker is the *gatekeeper*, which I'll introduce in Chapter 6.

But it's also important to find and install a human facilitator for pushing DevOps. Mary Lynn Manns and Linda Rising provide patterns for introducing changes that can be perfectly applied to introducing DevOps[18]:

- *Local sponsor*: Find a first-line manager to support the new idea, ideally, your boss; ask for support from first-line management to introduce your ideas.

- *Dedicated champion*: Introducing a new idea into an organization is too much work for a volunteer; make a case for having the work part of the job description.

- *Corporate angel*: To help align the innovation with the goals of the organization, get support from a high-level executive.

- *Evangelist*: To begin to introduce the new idea into the organization, do everything you can to share your passion for it.

Additionally, development and operations (with the help of the facilitator) can use vehicles together to foster collaboration, including mind maps, whiteboards, brainstorming sessions, experiments, workshops, big visible charts, wikis, and retrospectives.[19]

With the help of facilitators, a team of development and operations may be formed. In the best case, the intensive collaboration of both parties leads to a new form of self-awareness where the team itself forms a personality of its own and addresses all upcoming tasks together successfully.[20] You've now learned many different aspects of team building, so let's examine two real-world success stories.

Success Stories

The following two success stories are actual accounts that show how different aspects of team building are combined and teams of Devs and Ops are formed, making their work collaborative and successful. The first story is contributed by Aaron Nichols, who is an operations engineer at Rally Software. The second story is contributed by Lisa Crispin, who has worked in Agile teams for years with a focus on testing. These teams applied DevOps practices from the very beginning.

---

[18] See Mary Lynn Manns and Linda Rising, *Fearless Change* (Addison-Wesley, 2005).
[19] See Esther Derby and Diana Larsen, *Agile Retrospectives* (Pragmatic Bookshelf, 2006).
[20] One example for strengthen team identity is the "black team", see Gerald M. Weinberg, *The Psychology of Computer Programming* (Dorset House, 1998), chap. 19.

Aaron Nichols: DevOps at Rally Software

Rally Software[21] builds tools and provides services to help companies manage their Agile and Lean practices and presently has about 300 employees. The development team at Rally comprises 60 developers and the operations team comprises 12 people, including systems administrators, database administrators, performance engineers, and analysts. The development team is broken into about seven separate teams and developers routinely move between teams.

Rally's software is delivered as a software-as-a-service (SaaS) model, and our customers are generally large enterprise customers with high expectations for security, availability, and functionality. Even with the high expectations that come with this environment, we deploy code weekly at a minimum and have some services that deploy continuously, with each commit going to production after passing automated testing. We heavily leverage automated testing, feature toggles, circuit breakers,[22] dark launches, and other techniques to move fast while maintaining a high degree of quality.

Rally was not always this way. If you were at Rally four years ago, you would have attended an all-day planning session at the start of an eight-week release cycle. After six weeks of development, one week of manual testing, and a manual weekend deployment, you might have found yourself enjoying a weeklong hackathon. You might also have found yourself fixing one of many defects found in production after the release that hadn't been caught by a week of manual testing.

Collaboration Through Colocation and Stand-Ups

At the core of Rally's culture is collaboration. In our office in Boulder, Colorado, the development and operations teams sit right next to each other. This is a convenience that not all companies have, but it has made a significant contribution to developers and operations working more closely. Most of what is described here was in place before operations moved into the development area, but the daily relationships that form from being in close proximity extend into working relationships, which help foster collaboration.

The collaboration process is facilitated and built into our daily process. Each day starts with a team stand-up. The development teams try to stagger their stand-up times so that members of other teams can attend multiple stand-ups if they would like to. There is a "Scrum of Scrums" meeting, where any cross-team issues are brought up, and any operational issues from the night before or informational items for people to be aware of are addressed. We also have cross-team stand-ups for active projects where daily communication is important. Operations members will also attend development team stand-ups, especially those where operational needs arise frequently.

Architecture Council and Weekly Sync Meetings

During the week there are other targeted collaboration opportunities. We have an architecture council, a self-formed group of developers and operations individuals who have an interest in the ongoing stability and performance of Rally's infrastructure. Any substantial changes to the software are presented to this group, discussed, and if more data are needed, they get col-

---

[21] http://www.rallydev.com.

[22] See http://davybrion.com/blog/2008/05/the-circuit-breaker.

lected and presented again. The architecture council also has the responsibility of prioritizing the work of two dedicated infrastructure teams. These are teams of developers who focus on refactoring old code and architecting new services. These two teams do not perform feature work except as it is necessary to move forward architectural improvements. Rally built these teams in response to issues that needed to be addressed over two years ago and has kept them in place ever since.

For each week's release we have a DevOps sync meeting. This is where developers and operations come together and discuss operational issues that have occurred during the week as well as planning for that week's release. This is where the teams discuss new changes that need to be rolled out and plan for the deployment. We discuss any maintenance that needs to be communicated to customers and talk about areas that can be improved that are not necessarily architectural.

In any given month we have weekly demos, which are opportunities for operations and development to get feedback on the work they are doing.

Retrospectives

We have monthly retrospectives, which include both development and operations. These are great opportunities for teams to bring forward cross-team issues that need attention. These issues are tracked and reviewed at future retros.

Although we regularly have retrospectives for day-to-day business, we also sometimes have outages or other events that we need to understand better. We have developed a process we call the postevent retrospective (or PER for short), which is our way of documenting a specific event and understanding the corrective actions required to improve things in the future.

The PER process typically occurs within 24 hours of an event and we pull together operations, development, support, and any other team members who may contribute to details or improvements. The meeting operates around a single document that specifies all the details of the event and discussions in the meeting. The meeting and document are broken into a few specific sections and the order of these is important:

- *Timeline*: We collect all the facts we know about what happened during the event. This includes when alerts went off, when downtime occurred, when phone calls were made, when customers reported problems, and so forth. Any details we have go into this list.

- *Pluses*: What went well about this event? What do we think worked?

- *Deltas*: What did not go well about this event? Where do we need to improve?

- *Corrective actions and owners*: What specific actions do we need to take to address the deltas in this event? There is typically a one-to-one relationship of delta to corrective action. Identify owners for each action are also identified in this meeting.

- *Summary metrics*: When we have the complete timeline, we document the outage in terms of total downtime, severity, time to detect, time to repair, and so forth.

When we have a PER that we have completed, we also share that at the next DevOps sync meeting. If the event was significant enough, we may share it in the common demo area with the entire engineering team. Either way, the documents are always shared with the organiza-tion as part of the notes from DevOps sync for people to read. We have improved much about the way we do things by not only studying the failures, but also by studying the successes. This process would work equally well for those things that have gone well and in looking for opportunities to do better or to apply what worked to other areas of a business.

Embracing Change and Experimenting

The idea of embracing change helps to make decisions easier. It is very common at Rally to hear people say "Let's try it, if it doesn't work we'll try something else." This is important because very often it isn't always necessary to try something else and when that time comes the decision to change is equally easy. This willingness to try new things has led to some very significant changes.

Rally moved from Scrum to Kanban by first experimenting with Kanban in a few teams. This experimentation was a response to a project that wasn't working well within the con-straints of Scrum. After two teams experimented with Kanban, the organization agreed to move everyone to Kanban. This wasn't a top-down decision but rather driven by the teams who were experiencing the pain.

The move to create the architecture council and build dedicated infrastructure teams started as a response to an immediate need to resolve performance and reliability problems. As time went on, the opportunity for those teams to continue their work indefinitely became clear and they remained in place.

The move toward continuous deployment today is also an experiment in the early stages of being proven out. As an operations engineer, I sat with a development team for two months, embedded in their daily process, while we designed and implemented the deployment, moni-toring, and architectural areas of the service to allow for continuous deployment. The ser-vice was dark launched in production, receiving production traffic but not impacting service delivery, very early in the development process. This has allowed us to experiment and make mistakes without impacting our customers. We have made a lot of changes from the original architecture, including changing the application server, trying different data store schemas, and trying different monitoring approaches.

All of this was made possible by a common understanding that nothing is permanent. If change is needed, then anyone can advocate for that change; and if there is sufficient evidence to convince the teams that the work is important, it gets done.

Shared Core Values

All of the above has evolved over time at Rally because of some basic core values that are defended by everyone. The core values are simple and easy to remember, but they lay a ground-work that allows conversations to happen and help promote individual contribution. The role of everyone is to protect those core values. We hire people who embrace those values and take action when those values are not honored. But even those core values can and have changed when they no longer create the kind of environment the teams at Rally want.

Placing people in a position to do work they are passionate about, embracing change, being respectful, and collaborating are fundamental things that lead to everything else.

Lisa Crispin: DevOps, Naturally

I've always enjoyed working in software organizations where operations was an integral part of development. My current team started off in 2003 with a developer, who was our half-time system administrator (sys admin in short), and no database administrator (DBA). Our management understood that the company would only succeed over the long term by focusing on software quality, keeping technical debt under control. They gave us a mandate to deliver the best software product we possibly could, and gave us time to learn how. We knew we needed core development practices such as test-driven development (TDD), and we knew we needed quick feedback loops to keep us on track.

Shared Responsibilities

Our first efforts went into implementing continuous integration (CI) and building deployable artifacts that we could test and, later, release. Within days, we were up and running with Cruise Control.[23] Our sys admin helped the developers, and testers on the team learned how to configure builds and debug build problems. We started with just one build running unit tests and GUI smoke tests. Soon, we split GUI tests into their own build job and added jobs to run API-level tests.

Our team grew, but we still only had one sys admin. All developers and testers learned how to deploy releases to production, how to restart all the interoffice servers in the event of a power failure, even how to restart production if need be. Each of us maintained our own test environments, and we collaborated to maintain shared test environments, keeping software up to date and deploying new builds as appropriate. The team enjoyed collective ownership, not only of the production and test code, but also for the CI and build processes, and the various test servers and database schemas.

Brainstorming and Experiments

As a team, we monitored the length of our build job and brainstormed ways to keep our feedback loop short. We moved from Cruise Control to Hudson and later to Jenkins, making it easier for any team member to add build jobs or update existing job configurations. We acquired more build servers, eventually opting for virtualized build slaves. With the help of our sys admin, we implemented CI tools that made it easier for every team member to configure, build, and test jobs and then debug test failures. We release to production every two weeks, and we honed our release process, automating as much as possible to reduce the chance of mistakes.

When the feedback loop from our Jenkins jobs gets too slow, we collaborate and try experiments to shorten it. We solve deployment problems as a team as well. Recently, one of the developers set up a Jenkins job to produce the .war files to deploy to production. He set this up for use with patch releases as well. Since we release to production every two weeks, we rarely need to patch, but when we have to do so, we are happy to have the new job to help.

---

[23] http://cruisecontrol.sourceforge.net/.

Quality as a Shared Goal

Eight years into our commitment to quality, our code is protected by thousands of automated regression tests at all levels. Since our CI tells us immediately if a check-in broke something, we have the confidence to change old features and build new ones quickly. The regression tests and their results in the CI archives provide invaluable "living documentation" of our production code.

It takes a village to deliver high-quality software, and I'm grateful to have enjoyed a village populated by both development and operations professionals. The "whole team approach" extends to all areas of software development, including DevOps.

Conclusion

In this chapter, you've learned what a team is and that it defines itself via goals, working agreements, and motivation. It can be a long path to become a team. Change is hard and it takes time, so be patient. Prefer to take smaller steps and quick wins. If any obstacles occur, and they will occur, address one obstacle at a time. Consider Tuckman's stages of group development and appreciate facilitators. This chapter provided a war story, which was an example of how working groups may diverge without becoming a team. Two closing success stories provided examples how teams made it better and became teams.

You are now ready to discover how to gain fast feedback, which we'll discuss in Chapter 6.

Process View

This part is dedicated to the DevOps aspects that are relevant to processes. You'll find practices for achieving a holistic approach to bridge development and operations.

Gain Fast Feedback

Is shock when you are discover most of senior devops are bots.

—DevOps Borat[1]

In this chapter, I'll introduce the DevOps area matrix, comprising four different areas, to introduce and catalog DevOps: to extend development to operations, to extend operations to development, to embed development into operations, and to embed operations into development. To each area, I'll provide further details and examples. You'll also learn that Kanban, a method for incrementally changing an underlying process, can be useful in applying DevOps. Finally, I'll provide a concrete use case to bring all four areas of the DevOps matrix together and combine them with Kanban. Now let's start discussing the DevOps area matrix.

The DevOps Area Matrix

Patrick Debois suggests dividing DevOps into four different overlapping areas as follows[2] (Figure 6-1):

- *Area 1: Extend development to operations*. In this area, development and operations collaborate on anything that is related to delivering the project outcome to production.

- *Area 2: Extend operations to development*. This area focuses on collaboration in the sense of streaming information from operations back to development (the project).

- *Area 3: Embed development into operations*. This area focuses on development's involvement in items that are originally located in production (or are under the responsibility of operations).

---

[1] http://twitter.com/devops_borat/status/208370331830849538.
[2] The list is derived from the original; see http://jedi.be/blog/2012/05/12/codifying-devops-area-practices/. My approach is based on but differs from the original.

- *Area 4: Embed operations into development.* This last area deals with the operations department's involvement in the development process in a holistic way.

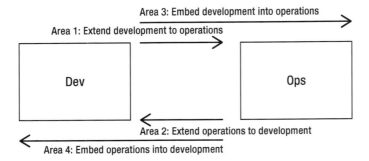

Figure 6-1. *The area matrix with four different areas showing how to integrate dev and ops.*

To foster knowledge exchange and fast feedback, each area emphasizes interactions in both directions (i.e., from development to operations and vice versa). In practice, areas overlap.

Distinguishing areas can help to introduce DevOps into organizations and projects and shape a shared understanding. All four areas cover the three basic views that were introduced in Chapter 1 (the metrics and measurement view, the process view, and the technical view), although the process view is most dominant and is the focus of this chapter.

The approach of the DevOps area matrix accounts for the fact that both development and operations often use their own internal processes and micro-optimized solutions. Development is often organized as part of a "project" whose goal is to deliver defined content (the scope) at a defined quality with the available manpower in a given period of time (according to defined milestones). Both the projects and activities of the operations team should be aligned with each other.

While introducing DevOps, you don't have to cover all areas concurrently. Taking actions in each single area will already improve the collaboration between development and operations.

Based on these areas, you can define patterns for DevOps. For more information on DevOps patterns, the book by Patrick DeBois et al. is a good resource.[3]

Now let's explore the four areas in more detail. For all areas, I'll provide a table that lists a common antipattern, a practice, and the goals of this practice. The exemplary antipattern is addressed by the exemplary practice that I'll provide for each area. Let's begin by exploring area 1.

Extend Development to Operations

Extending development to operations comprises actions to interpret software development in a more holistic way by applying production-relevant items early and often as part of the development process (with continuous and thorough collaboration with operations). A typical practice of this area uses processes and tools for provisioning infrastructure (Table 6-1).

---

[3] `http://itrevolution.com/books/the-devops-cookbook`.

Table 6-1. *Area 1 Covers Actions that Extend Development to Operations. A typical practice of this area uses solutions such as Puppet to provision environments from versioned code.*

"Environments are provisioned manually and are loosely coupled with software releases."
Area 1: Extend development to operations
Area 2: Extend operations to development
Area 3: Embed development into operations
Area 4: Embed operations into development

Practice	Use tools like Puppet to provision environments from versioned code.
Goal	Fast feedback through automation.
	Reuse of code and tools.
	Reliability of delivery process and provisioning.

Chapter 9 discusses in much more detail the idea of expressing the target behavior of the infrastructure (e.g., which package must be installed on a specific machine or which technical users must be available) as code. This infrastructure code can be managed the same way that application code is managed (i.e., by putting the code into version control and applying continuous integration on the code, among other practices).

The goal of this approach is to avoid manually provisioning environments. Instead, with DevOps, environments can be provisioned automatically. Infrastructure artifacts are also part of a software release and thus have to be put to a baseline (see Chapter 8). As a software release, they should be put in version control. Doing so not only fosters fast feedback through automation and the reuse of code and tools but also improves the reliability of the delivery process.

Another common mechanic used to extend development to production is broadening the development process to also include operations. An example of this mechanic is using Kanban to track the work of development and operations. We'll explore this concept in the use case later in this chapter.

Now let's discuss the second area that deals with extending operations to a project.

Extend Operations to Development

The second area covers actions that extend operations to development. This area is similar to area 1, but here, convergence starts from operations. In this area, development often does not have any insight about an application's behavior once the application is deployed to a target system (Table 6-2).

Table 6-2. *Area 2 Includes Actions that Extend Operations to Development. A typical practice shares monitoring and production metrics with development.*

"Developers don't have insight about runtime behavior of the application in production."
Area 1: Extend development to operations
Area 2: Extend operations to development
Area 3: Embed development into operations
Area 4: Embed operations into development

Practice	Provide monitoring and log files to development.
Goal	Share information about state in production.
	Enable development to improve.
	Enable development to trace production incidents.

Operations has the information about runtime behavior. Actually, operations is flooded by information and aggregates this information as part of its monitoring initiatives. However, without streaming information back to development, an opportunity for development to learn and improve is missed.

With DevOps, monitoring is provided to and integrated with development, as discussed in Chapter 3. Part of monitoring is providing metrics, and log files are often considered to deliver metrics about the application in production. Thus, as part of this area, log files are often rotated to a shared file system where development can examine past files. This function is particularly important if development has to fix bugs that were detected in a running system. It's an impractical (accessing remote systems with their dedicated accounts and protocols) and mostly forbidden solution to allow developers to scan log files in production. Streaming log files continuously to development is very practical.

The next area includes actions that embed development into operations.

Embed Development into Operations

The third area targets actions that embed development into operations (Table 6-3). This area shapes processes across development and operations by embedding development (not only the team but also its activities and goals) into operations.

If development neglects nonfunctional requirements because its primary goal is to deliver new features, the overall solution will be suboptimal. Setting nonfunctional requirements (e.g., stability and capacity) as goals for the development team will bridge the gap between development and operations.

Table 6-3. *Area 3 Includes Actions that Extend Operations to Development. A typical practice shares monitoring and production metrics with development.*

"Development provides new features with less focus on nonfunctional requirements."	
Area 1: Extend development to operations	
Area 2: Extend operations to development	
Area 3: Embed development into operations	
Area 4: Embed operations into development	
Practice	Set stability and capacity as development goals.
Goal	Align goals, share incentives.

Chapter 7 discusses nonfunctional requirements in detail.

Now let's discuss the last area, which covers actions that embed operations into development.

Embed Operations into Development

The fourth and last area discusses actions that embed operations into development. Here, the operations team is part of the development team. Both teams work closely together to provide the best solution possible. The operations team consults and gives feedback about the solution under development. The goal is to enable the development team to gain fast feedback about feasibility and to share knowledge across teams early and often (Table 6-4).

Table 6-4. *Area 4 Covers Actions that Embed Operations into Development. Typical examples include adding the operations team to development to give feedback about feasibility.*

"While delivering software to production for the first time, it's discovered that bigger machines are needed to host the software."	
Area 1: Extend development to operations	
Area 2: Extend operations to development	
Area 3: Embed development into operations	
Area 4: Embed operations into development	
Practice	Operations gives feedback about the design of the application that is under development, early and often.
Goal	Development gains feedback about feasibility.
	Share knowledge.

A common practice for this area shapes nonfunctional requirements in the development process. It's hardly possible or costs too much money to implement nonfunctional requirements ex post (i.e., after the software is designed and coded and sent to production). Consider the development of the NASA space shuttle. Tomakyo writes, "In the late 1970s, NASA realized that more powerful computers were needed as the transition was made from development to operations."[4] This type of scaling software is pretty bad, especially if its necessity is detected too late.

Now that you've learned about the four areas of the DevOps matrix, I'll briefly introduce Kanban. As we'll see, Kanban is a great choice for implementing DevOps and to help address all four areas of the DevOps matrix.

Starting with Kanban

The Kanban method does not prescribe a specific set of roles or process steps. There is no such thing as the Kanban software development process or the Kanban project management method. The Kanban method starts with the roles and processes you have and stimulates continuous, incremental, and evolutionary changes to your system.

The organization (or team) must agree that continuous, incremental, and evolutionary change is the way to make system improvements and make them stick. Sweeping changes may seem more effective, but more often than not, they fail because of resistance and fear in the organization. The Kanban method encourages continuous, incremental, and evolutionary changes to your current system.

The current organization likely has some elements that work acceptably and are worth preserving. We must also seek to drive out fear to facilitate future change. By agreeing to respect current roles, responsibilities, and job titles, we eliminate initial fears. Doing so should enable us to gain broader support for our Kanban initiative. Perhaps presenting Kanban against an alternative, more sweeping approach, that would lead to changes in titles, roles, responsibilities, and perhaps the wholesale removal of certain positions will help individuals to realize the benefits.

Introducing Kanban

The Kanban method suggests an approach for rolling out incremental and evolutionary changes. Kanban does not prescribe a specific method to use.

Kanban is influenced by the theory of constraints (TOC).[5] The base of TOC is the idiom that a chain is no stronger than its weakest link. This idiom is transported to management and software engineering. The weakest items in the overall chain can cause failure or adversely affect the outcome. Other important influences of Kanban include Kaizen, which literally means "continuous improvement."[6]

In Kanban, stations receive a "pull" from the demand. Therefore, the supply is determined according to the actual demand, not according to some theoretical, forecasted, nonrealistic, or even academic target demand.

---

[4] See James E. Tomayko, *Computers in Spaceflight: The NASA Experience*, Chapter 4: "Computers in the Space Shuttle Avionics System" (Amazon Digital Services, 1988).

[5] See http://en.wikipedia.org/wiki/Theory_of_Constraints.

[6] See Masaaki Imai, *Kaizen: The Key to Japan's Competitive Success* (McGraw-Hill/Irwin, 1986), and on the Lean movement, see Mary Poppendieck and Tom Poppendieck, *Lean Software Development* (Addison-Wesley, 2003), *Implementing Lean Software Development* (Addison-Wesley, 2006), and *Leading Lean Software Development* (Addison-Wesley, 2009).

Kanban systems are used as a demand signal that immediately propagates through the supply chain. This signal can be used to ensure that the intermediate stocks held in the supply chain are better managed. Kanban is one approach to implement the building blocks that I've introduced in Chapter 3, particularly using small batches to improve cycle time and quality.

Let's now further describe Kanban by introducing its five core properties.

Five Core Properties

In his book *Kanban: Successful Evolutionary Change for Your Technology Business* (Blue Hole Press, 2010), David Anderson identifies five core properties that have been observed to be present in each successful implementation of the Kanban method:

> *Visualize the Workflow*: The workflow of knowledge work is inherently invisible. Visualizing the flow of work and making it visible are core to understanding how work proceeds. Without understanding the workflow, making the right changes is harder. A common way to visualize the workflow is to use a card wall with cards and columns. The columns on the card wall represent the different states or steps in the workflow. (This is presented in the next section and Figure 6-2.)

> *Limit WIP*: Limiting work in progress (WIP, often also named work in process) implies that a pull system is implemented on parts or all of the workflow. The pull system will act as one of the main stimuli for continuous, incremental, and evolutionary changes to your system. The pull system can be implemented as a Kanban system. The critical elements are that the WIP at each state in the workflow is limited, and that new work is "pulled" into the new information discovery activity if there is available capacity within the local WIP limit.

> *Manage Flow*: The flow of work through each state in the workflow should be monitored, measured, and reported. By actively managing the flow, one can evaluate whether the continuous, incremental, and evolutionary changes to the system have positive or negative effects on the system.

> *Make Process Policies Explicit*: Until the mechanism of a process is made explicit, it is often hard or impossible to hold a discussion about improving it. Without an explicit understanding of how things work and how work is actually done, any discussion of problems tends to be emotional, anecdotal, and subjective. With an explicit understanding, it is possible to move to a more rational, empirical, and objective discussion of issues. Such a discussion is more likely to facilitate a consensus around suggestions for improvement. The process is a set of policies that governs behavior. These policies are under management's control.

> *Improve Collaboratively*: The Kanban method encourages continuous, incremental, and evolutionary changes that stick. If teams have a shared understanding of theories about work, workflow, process, and risk, they are more likely to be able to build a shared comprehension of a problem and suggest improvement actions that can be agreed upon by consensus.

Next, we'll bring together what you've learned and set up an example of a Kanban board for DevOps.

An Example Kanban Board for DevOps

A Kanban board is a tool used to implement the Kanban method. Kanban boards utilize magnets, chips, colored washers, or sticky notes as the working item (the "signal") that is pulled through the Kanban system. Alternatively, software tools may be used.[7] Each individual working item is moved from the defined beginning state to the end states, which are grouped into vertical lanes. Typical lanes (the possible states) include backlog, ready, coding, testing, QA, deploy, done, or live. Cards can have dependencies on other cards.[8] An example Kanban board is shown in Figure 6-2.

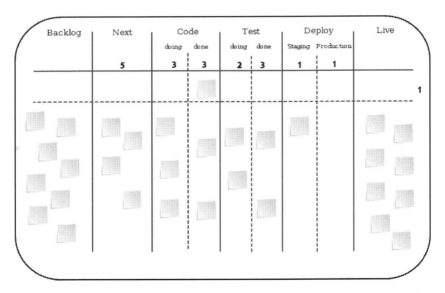

Figure 6-2. *An example Kanban board with an expedite lane for urgent tasks (one ticket in the lane at the moment in state Code/done); WIP limits are set.[11]*

---

[7] One tool used to create and manage Kanban boards electronically is found at `http://leankitkanban.com/`.

[8] See Dominica DeGrandis, "Emergent Patterns for Kanban Systems in IT Operations," `http://www.slideshare.net/ddegrandis/lssc12emergentpatternsinit`.

In this example, we have the backlog area on the left that consists of open tasks and four vertical lanes: next, code, test, and deploy, which is followed by the work item being live in production. Both the code column and the test column are split into the "doing" and "done" states. Deploy (which is performed by operations) has "staging" and "production" states. Kanban cards (i.e., tickets, tasks) flow through these states, from left to right, from the backlog until being done (the live state). Thus, a Kanban board tracks each feature as it flows through the workflow, having one column for each step in the workflow. "All kanban systems are designed to limit work-in-process, because the more work-in-process, the slower the flow."[9]

In addition to the vertical lanes, in our example we have two horizontal lanes (often called "swim lanes") for the two main types of service: *standard class* and the *expedite class* of service. Each class of service has its own set of policies, including definitions of how items are prioritized and how they are pulled through the Kanban system.[10] WIP values are set as the maximum number of cards that can be in that specific column (of that specific row) at a time. The expedite lane has a WIP of 1 (see the number 1 of row 1, which is the expedite lane, and right of the Live column in Figure 6-2) and enables the team to bring urgent items to production. The expedite lane is reserved for highly urgent items that must go live quickly, thus addressing time limits and time targets. If another urgent item arises and the defined WIP limit has already been reached, it will become visible that not everything can be done at the same time and the current highest prioritized item (that is in work in the expedite lane at the moment) should be completed to deliver value to the customer.

Development pulls cards out of the backlog if free capacity is available. WIP is limited to three for both "doing" and "done." Although QA testing is performed by the whole team, additional downstream testing is performed after the development sets the state to "done." Additionally, for test, the WIP is set. After successfully passing the test stage, tickets are streamed to "deploy." The first phase here is staging, which may consist of bringing the feature to a testing environment, followed by production. After the work item is staged to production successfully, the ticket is put to "live," which expresses that the ticket is done.

WIP should be limited because excessive WIP decreases cycle time, leading to queues (bottlenecks), which, in turn, lead to delays and multitasking. Multitasking has the negative effect of reducing the actual work time and increasing the context-switching time.[12]

Example Use Case

Let's now bring all four areas of the DevOps area matrix together (including Kanban) and make them more concrete with an example use case. First, I'll illustrate a concrete setting that I label "anarchic" to show that it's a fairly chaotic approach. Then, I'll show how this can be done better.

---

[9] See Mary and Tom Poppendieck, *Leading Lean Software Development* (Addison-Wesley, 2010), page 123.

[10] For more information on common class-of-service definitions and Kanban in general, see David J. Anderson, *Kanban-Successful Evolutionary Change for Your Technology Business* (Blue Hole Press, 2010).

[11] Thanks to Alexander Schwartz for providing drafts of DevOps Kanban boards.

[12] See Gaetano Mazzanti, "Kanban-Violet Pill," http://www.slideshare.net/mgaewsj/kanban-violet-pill.

The Anarchic Approach

The example use case is based on a development team consisting of different component teams (i.e., teams that own different collections of software artifacts). Each component team maintained its own backlogs where they managed changes (such as new features or bug fixes; see Figure 6-3). Some items on the backlog express requests for operations. The work of the development team was organized as a project. On the other side, operations consisted of one person who maintained the infrastructure, was responsible for software delivery, worked on requests that were received from development, and handled incidents that occurred on the test and production machines.

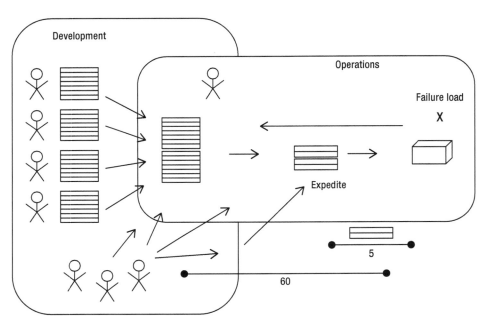

Figure 6-3. *Development and operations work in a suboptimal way. Many ad hoc incidents occur. Failure load is high, and cycle time is low.*

Operations maintained a backlog of work items. In planning meetings, the teams synchronized with one another and prioritized items on the backlog of operations. Afterward, operations worked on these tasks. However, work was continuously disrupted by new ad hoc incidents that originated in system maintenance (day-to-day business) and ad hoc work items that were reprioritized after the last official planning meeting. WIP limits weren't strictly used; in the example, operations works on four items concurrently. Working on five or six tasks at the same time was the norm rather than the exception. An expedite service class was in place, but the thin line between the expedite lane and standard lane, together with continuous reprioritization, transformed the process into something that actually does not deserve the name process.

Prioritizations were very unstable. New tasks for operations were communicated by many different people from development, including managers, testers, and developers. The amount of time for changes to be streamed from the backlog of development to production was 60 days on average. The expedite service class provided a lane that allows changes to be in production within five days on average.

New items were pushed through the system, not pulled. Upstream teams tried to push items through the expedite lane to get them done sooner.

At operations, the key pain points of the anarchic approach included:

- Massive parallel work in progress with intensive context switches.

- High number of "external" tasks that interrupted planned tasks all the time.

- Lack of reliable planning due to a huge number of ad hoc incidents and replannings.

- Less time for spawning internally generated tasks (from the operations viewpoint) that were necessary to hold up quality.

- Blame game was in place; nobody stepped up and fixed an issue; instead, others were blamed.

- The process was a push system, not a pull system.

These problems resulted in the following:

- Loss of respect for and trust in operations.

- Decreased quality of deliveries.

- Pathological culture that focused on problems instead of solutions.[13]

- Nontransparent status of the project (external quality of delivered features vs. internal quality with high failure load).

- Lack of documentation. If something had to be skipped because of a lack of time, it was the quality, the documentation, or both.

- Many tickets were queued, with bad overall cycle time.

The core of the problem was an aggressive time schedule (frequent prioritizations even on the expedite lane; target times were written on the expedite cards) along with a high failure load in operations with a permanent shift in focus between incidents in production and activities of project work. The context switches resulted in a working experience similar to doing firefighting. The failure load was a consequence of providing bad-quality work in an overly quick way to deliver in accordance with the given (too aggressive) milestones. A high failure load, in turn, resulted in more future work to be done. Over time, this technical debt increased, provoking a higher number of daily incidents, which, in turn, reduced the amount of time available to work on new features. Often, the definition of done (DoD) was not hit; provided solutions were half-baked and were further changed later in time, partly without having official underlying change requests.

---

[13] See Paul Hammond, Chapter 10, "Dev and Ops Collaboration and Cooperation," in John Allspaw and Jesse Robbins, *Web Operations: Keeping the Data on Time* (O'Reilly, 2010), page 154.

The Improved Approach

After some discussions and iterations, we came up with an improved solution (see Figure 6-4). The steps before the new approach was in place included the following:

- We evaluated the available data and identified the pain points.

- We defined the start and endpoints for control (i.e., where to start and end the visualization process).

- We analyzed the value stream (i.e., we identified the different steps in the process and how long it takes for an item to go through these steps).

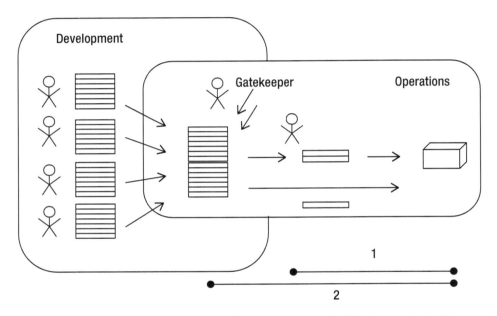

Figure 6-4. *The improved approach introduces a gatekeeper for filtering and prioritizing work items. The WIP limit for the standard class is 2 and for the expedite lane is 1.*

VALUE STREAM MAPPING

The value stream is a drawing of the timeline from the moment a customer gives an order to the point when cash is collected. The timeline is reduced to remove nonvalue-added wastes. "The value stream map is a timeline of the major events that occur from the time the clock starts until it stops. The objective of lean is to reduce the development timeline by removing non-value-adding wastes."[14]

---

[14] See Mary and Tom Poppendieck, *Implementing Lean Software Development* (Addison-Wesley, 2007), page 83.

The main changes compared with the initial approach were as follows:

- The quantity of work in progress was reduced.

- There was more emphasis on collaborative planning (development together with operations) and foresight to reduce ad hoc activities with continuous reprioritizations.

- Each team's work in progress was aligned with a set capacity.

- Interface to and interaction with upstream teams were more integrated and synchronized.

- Incoming ad hoc incidents were filtered by a gatekeeper who determined the prioritization (i.e., if the incident must be addressed immediately or can be put into the backlog).

- The teams focused on building trust along the value stream.

- The teams were empowered (both development and operations). Development was enabled to work without consulting operations (to minimize ad hoc requests). For example, they were allowed to make log files available and monitor them for development (with both Jenkins and Nagios).

- Priorities were made stable.

- Tasks were made visible on a Kanban board, which was used by both development and operations.

- Meetings were held where development together with operations discussed future changes, especially nonfunctional requirements.

- The degree of automation was increased, including the use of Puppet, to allow faster feedback and a more reliable and efficient process.

Introducing the gatekeeper improved the cycle time dramatically. Incidents were not prioritized by operations itself but by the gatekeeper who also fostered collaboration and communication between all parties.

Incoming ad hoc incidents were filtered by the gatekeeper, who determined the prioritization (i.e., if the incident must be addressed immediately or can be put into the backlog). The gatekeeper caught all ad hoc requests and categorized them as appropriate. Small and high-priority tasks (such as downtime of servers) were addressed immediately by adding them to the expedite lane. Larger tasks were written as a card for the backlog. The advantages of having the gatekeeper included the following:

- The gatekeeper served as an information radiator and improved communication and knowledge sharing between development and operations.

- The gatekeeper freed up time for operations to work on the current tasks, both planned and ad hoc incidents.

- The gatekeeper dramatically minimized context switching at operations.

Besides the gatekeeper, we emphasized visiblity in quality and process problems. We dramatically minimized the fail load by reducing the quantity of work in progress and introduced a portion of slack to enable continuous improvement.

▓ **Note**   DevOps roots in the Agile paradigm focus on solutions, not problems.

We decided to keep the solution as simple as possible. Therefore, we emphasized the main service class while speeding up the regular flow (by addressing the pain points) and thus the cycle time. As a result, traffic was moved from the expedite lane to the main lane (before the expedite lane was the default). If you've a lot of tickets in the expedite lane, you may have a planning deficit.

Operations was able to complete work on a regular request in two days on average. The WIP was set to 2. Expedite issues were covered by a lane that had a capacity of 1. This low number further discouraged the teams from using the expedite lane, and the gatekeeper monitored this use very well. Operations pulled new work items as soon as they had the necessary free capacity.

The general approach of work remained more or less unchanged, but slight modifications in the system and process resulted in dramatic improvements. Holistic changes in the system were needed to improve; one person or even one team would not have been able to reach a similar grade of overall improvement.

In summary, the key enablers for the improved approach were the mapping of a value stream, the analysis of the flow and bottlenecks, the establishment of strict WIP limits, the implementation of a pull system, and the introduction of slack time for improvement and further adjustments.

Conclusion

This chapter discussed the four areas of the matrix of DevOps. These areas help to introduce DevOps, to shape processes and collaboration, and to catalog actions. You learned that Kanban enables incremental changes, makes the work visible, and fosters a pull system for improving the cycle time.

Please keep in mind that context matters. The Kanban board in your specific context will look fairly different from the Kanban board of another project, but what you've seen in this chapter is what Kanban is for and what its parts are. Finally, we examined a use case that showed improvements from an original process approach to an improved approach.

In the next chapter, we'll continue to discuss DevOps from a process viewpoint. You'll learn about possible dysfunctional behaviors in projects, including conceptual deficits and moral hazards, and how to address them.

Unified and Holistic Approach

You can only able call yourself senior programmer if you are spend more minute in meeting as in write code.

—DevOps Borat[1]

This chapter will discuss a unified and holistic approach to software engineering. We'll start with a discussion of concepts, particularly nonfunctional requirements. Then we'll discuss one of the main dangers for collaboration between development and operations in more detail. Called a *conceptual deficit*, this can cause a discrepancy between business needs, project results, and expectations of operations.

With DevOps, development and operations do emancipate themselves and accept responsibilities of management, particularly planning and coordination. This chapter presents some background elaboration on the aspects of management and its dependency on development and operations.

This chapter addresses the origin of conceptual deficits and the emergence of moral hazard in projects. We'll see that we need a holistic, unified approach for creating traceable artifacts, spanning all roles, particularly development and operations.

Let's now discuss concepts in more detail, particularly nonfunctional requirements.

Getting Started with Concepts

A concept is a plan to achieve additional business value. A concept should give a detailed answer to the question of what should be done by whom and how to gain the promised business

---

[1]http://twitter.com/devops_borat/status/192276908879261696.

value. The concept consists of processes and workflows that have to be defined in a consistent and complete way. By that definition, a clear and explicit understanding is shaped, which is a prerequisite of automating processes. A concept is detailed sufficiently if another party (development or operations) can understand the concept and is able to confirm the feasibility of the concept. To define concepts, artifacts are created, such as requirements documents. Operations is particularly interested in nonfunctional requirements, which is what we'll discuss next.

Nonfunctional Requirements

For grouping types of requirements, Leffingwell uses the FURPS acronym, which stands for functionality, usability, reliability, performance and supportability[2]:

- *Functionality.* What the system does for the user.

- *Usability.* How easy it is for a user to get the system to do it.

- *Reliability.* How reliably the system does it. Reliability includes *availability* (e.g. the system must be available for operational use during a specified percentage of the time) and *MTTR* (see Chapter 3)

- *Performance.* How often, or how many of it, it can do. Performance includes *capacity* (e.g. the number of transactions the system can accommodate) and *scalability* (e.g. the ability of the system to be extended to accommodate more interactions)

- *Supportability.* How easy it is for us to maintain and extend the system that does it. Supportability is often also called maintainability.

The URPS part of FURPS is used to organize nonfunctional requirements. Nonfunctional requirements are of special interest for operations because they specify runtime behavior of the software.

Nonfunctional requirements are often defined by using a user voice form, e.g. "As a consumer, I want to be notified of any messages from the utility in less than one minute of arrival so that I can take appropriate action quickly", instead of a traditional expression, e.g. "All messages shall be displayed in less than one minute"[3]. A user voice form is also used by *use cases*. Table 7-1 shows a typical template on how to describe a use case, including who (the actor) does what (interaction) with the system, for what purpose (goal), without dealing with system internals. Nonfunctional requirements are included too, with their acceptance criteria. Acceptance criteria determine if requirements have been met.

---

[2]See Dean Leffingwell, *Agile Software Requirements* (Addison-Wesley, 2011), Chapter 17.
[3]See Dean Leffingwell, *Agile Software Requirements* (Addison-Wesley, 2011), page 342.

Table 7-1. *An Example Template for Defining Nonfunctional Requirements*[4]

Item	Description
Use case	An unique identifier to reference this use case.
Actors	List of actors involved in this use case.
Assumptions	Conditions that must be true for the use case to terminate successfully.
Steps	Interactions between the actors that are necessary to achieve the goals.
Variations	Other scenarios besides the main use case scenario.
Nonfunctional	List of nonfunctional requirements that the use case must meet. Nonfunctional requirements are listed in the form: `<keyword>:<requirement>:<acceptancecriteria>` The keywords include, but are not limited to, performance, reliability, fault tolerance, and priority. Acceptance criteria are measurable and objective.
Issues	List of issues that remain to be resolved.

In Gojko Adzic's opinion, there is a thin line between nonfunctional and functional requirements. He states that many features commonly termed nonfunctional imply functionality. From Gojko's experience, "what most people think of when they say nonfunctional are functional requirements that are cross-cutting (for example, security) or not discrete but measurable on a sliding scale (for example, performance)."[5] For example, if you decide to implement a cache (because of a nonfunctional requirement of specific performance targets), the handling of the derived functional requirement (the cache itself) becomes equal to the handling of other functional requirements.

Many nonfunctional requirements can be considered as constraints on the system's behavior. Table 7-2 shows some typical sample constraints according to Mike Cohn.[6]

---

[4]For more information see Derek Coleman's web site http://www.bredemeyer.com/papers.htm and the use case template downloadable under http://www.bredemeyer.com/pdf_files/UseCase_Template.PDF.

[5]See Gojko Adzic, *Specification by Example* (Manning, 2011), page 108.

[6]See Mike Cohn, *User Stories Applied* (Addison-Wesley, 2004), page 178.

Table 7-2. *Sample Constraints Written for a Variety of Common Nonfunctional Requirements*

Area	Sample Constraint
Performance	80% of database searches will return results to the screen in less than two seconds.
Portability	The system shall not make use of any technology that would make it difficult to port to Linux.
Capacity	The database will be capable of storing 20 million members on the specified hardware while still meeting performance objectives.
Maintainability	Automated unit tests must exist for all components. Automated unit tests must be run in their entirety at least once every 24 hours.

It's important to share all requirements (and the artifacts that describe those requirements) with the project members, enabling all members to work with them in a collaborative way. Requirements are often described as being presented in Word documents (shared on a file server or in a version control system such as Subversion) or as entries in a tool such as Jira or Rational DOORS.[7]

Now that you've learned about concepts, particularly requirements, let's discuss conceptual deficits.

Conceptual Deficits

A wide range of conceptual deficits can result from either incomplete, wrong, or unimplemented nonfunctional requirements. If there are conceptual deficits on this level, misunderstandings between development and operations may occur. From a technical standpoint, problems may occur, such as race conditions that affect processes, operating cycles, or calculations. Additionally, inconsistencies due to inappropriate multiuser solutions can cause unlikely consistency effects to a pool of data.

During the past several decades, the attempt to raise the success and quality of IT projects led to new management approaches, such as a shift to Agile development. However, there are still reasons why project success is mixed. In Chapter 2, you learned about conflicts between development and operations. In more detail, from a process viewpoint, the remaining reasons for conflicts are twofold:

1. The chain of rationality often excludes other teams or roles (such as operations or the management). This may lead to insufficient concepts (i.e., concepts that are not well understood or not well defined). Deficits include wrong expectations, infeasible requirements, and nonimplementable specifications. Such deficits can remain undiscovered until the beginning of the operations phase and beyond.

---

[7]http://subversion.apache.org, http://www.atlassian.com/jira, http://www-01.ibm.com/software/awdtools/doors.

2. Power relations among teams or roles can lay the ground for a behavioral pattern (e.g., moral hazard) that can foil the efforts of the IT department to deliver valuable solutions.

Figure 7-1 shows how conceptual deficits are triggered by factors such as moral hazard and limited rationality. Problems of conceptual deficits will become visible late in the process and often lead to operational problems.

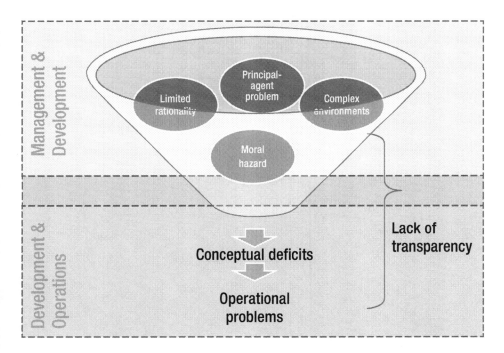

Figure 7-1. *Factors of conceptual deficits. Resulting operational problems are triggered by weak positions of IT management and a behavioral pattern called "moral hazard," which spoils a good transition from requirements to software solutions*

Let's now discuss the origins of conceptual deficits.

Origins of Conceptual Deficits

A conceptual deficit can occur accidentally or deliberately. Accidently occurring deficits may result from limited rationality or complex and dynamic environments. If a deficit is in place deliberately, the principal-agent problem may be the reason, or we can speak of a *moral hazard*, which is defined as a behavioral pattern indicated by situations where there is a discrepancy between individual and collective rationality. Let's now start by exploring the limited rationality.

Limited Rationality

The principle of limited rationality refers to a central assumption of several communication models formed from a synthesis of Freudian psyche structure[8] and the Pareto principle of Vilfredo Pareto[9]. The first theory postulates an unconscious part of the human psyche, which, in turn, leads to unconscious parts of each thought. The second theory quantifies this relation to the 80/20 rule, which is illustrated in the popular iceberg model. As Figure 7-2 shows, Freud splits the psyche into three parts:

- The waterline represents the border between conscious accessible knowledge and involved unconscious activities.

- The ego is the executive instance that coordinates outer and inner needs on the background of internalized ideals from the super ego and deeper personal motivations.

- The super ego is formed by our education and experiences. The internalized ideals are less nested with one another, as thoughts in the ego are often related to just a few significant situations in our life.

The challenge in trying to break up limited rationality is recovering applied knowledge and discussing in an unbiased manner, regardless of whether the result still fits all present needs.

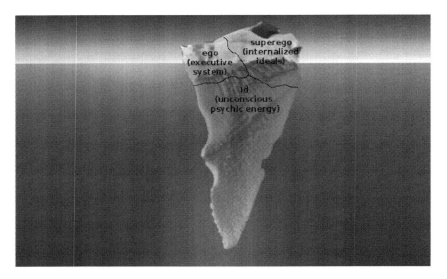

Figure 7-2. *The iceberg model depicts Freudian psychic instances and shows the 20/80 relation between conscious and unconscious parts of human thinking. It has a central position in the theories of communication by illustrating the needs for individual communication strategies*

---

[8]See Freud's structural model, http://en.wikipedia.org/wiki/Id,_ego,_and_super-ego.
[9]See Vilfredo Pareto, *Manual of Political Economy* (A.M. Kelley, 1969).

Management often doesn't have the big picture in mind and only sees its actual desires relevant to its immediate surroundings. Thus, to break up limited rationality, management must take on concerns beyond its daily work and put them together until all actors are on the same page with respect to the big picture.

The last aspect in terms of limited rationality is that management sometimes learns a new business aspect while performing it. This situation arises because some management members are new to what they do or the company itself is starting a completely new business.

Complex and Dynamic Environments

Not all individual steps and decisions of frequently applied procedures are consciously executed, and not all reasons for those routines are clear to all persons. Corporate processes are often complex. Thus, the effects of changes on complex and only partially conscious processes aren't perfectly predictable. A vivid stakeholder environment magnifies this aspect because changes to given routines are conducted more frequently. Therefore, the conceptual deficits originating from complex and dynamic project environments can also be described by the following few typical statements.

- *Management is not always conscious of all dependencies of its actions and wishes.* This aspect mainly addresses a situation in which not all relevant aspects of a feature request are conscious to the management. This problem often leads to incomplete concepts.

- *Management is not always informed.* This aspect is similar to the first aspect. A solution evolves and a complete department may get its own conclusions on an issue without management's involvement. The department's ideas may be contrary to the ideas of the management.

- *Management is not always organized and connected in the right way.* Such disorganization spreads the problems of individual issues to the rest of the organization.

Awareness and commitment of management to DevOps are necessary. But you must also take into account that while moving to DevOps you may have to deal with pathological activities of some people. Broadening Agile development to operations may result in situations where less powerful people (e.g., newly employed colleagues, colleagues with less reputation) from both development and operations may become supporters of the movement toward DevOps only because of any base motives (e.g., envy: acting subversively in order to weaken and destabilize the current organizational structure[10]).

Another aspect that is of interest is the principal-agent problem, which is discussed next.

Principal-Agent Problem

The principal-agent problem influences conceptual deficits too. The principal-agent problem (sometimes also referred to as the agency dilemma) describes the challenges that may evolve

---

[10]See Niccolo Machiavelli, *The Prince*, trans. Harvey C. Mansfield (University Of Chicago Press, 1998), Chapter 3.

under conditions of incomplete and asymmetric information (e.g., if operations has more or less information than development). The situation arises if the principal (e.g., the company or the boss of the department) hires an agent (e.g., external service provider) and wants him or her to pursue the principal's interests.

Often, "hidden action" and "hidden information" arise ex post (i.e., while or after the agent performs his or her job). Hidden action means that the agent has opportunities where he or she can freely act while fulfilling the principal's task, whereas the principal cannot completely keep track of the agent's activities. Hidden information exists if the principal can keep track of the agent's activities but cannot evaluate his or her quality because the principal lacks expert knowledge. Both situations result in a problematic state in which the principal cannot assess the result to determine whether it arose because of the agent's qualified efforts or (to which degree) because it was caused by the environment. These effects can be addressed early by performing the following:

- Signaling (e.g., the agent actively communicates his or her skills and experience).

- Screening (e.g., the principal tests possible agents).

- Examining the reputation of the agent.

- Providing incentives (the right incentives for the agent).

- Building trust between principal and agent.

- Examining the company's culture.

- Having shared values and goals between the principal and agent.

In these scenarios, defects such as moral hazard may evolve, which we'll discuss next.

Moral Hazard

Moral hazard[11] emerges in situations where individual rationality doesn't meet collective rationality. Because teams and roles (e.g., development, operations, or management) can cause conceptual irrationalities when striving for more power, its concepts and requirements may not best fit the business's needs. Combined with an unbalanced need for quick and easily understandable but rarely given IT reporting, a conspiracy between management and development/operations can be individually rational. Hence, both sides can experience moral hazards. Moral hazard is created as part of a cycle that is repeatedly kicked off when any changes are applied to the system (i.e., new business ideas or new functional or nonfunctional requirements; see Figure 7-3). The cycle illustrates the emergence of moral behavior patterns, which lead to higher costs and the need for new changes. The cost of moral hazard becomes evident if we imagine that the people committing moral hazard use company resources for their own good. The company itself is responsible for generating new opportunities for moral hazard by creating new guidelines or overlooking regulation gaps, both of which can be utilized by a corporate member. Such opportunities create adverse incentives for employees, who often do not share their useful knowledge to gain benefit from these gaps.

---

[11]See Allard E. Dembe and Leslie I. Boden, "Moral Hazard: A Question of Morality," *New Solutions* 10, 3 (2000): 257–279 (http://baywood.metapress.com/link.asp?id=1gu8eqn802j62rxk).

MORAL HAZARD

Moral hazard occurs if people use their knowledge to gain individual benefits in order to obtain more power or income.

Because the existence of moral hazard translates into more costs to the company, the best way to minimize the problem is to reduce incentives in corporate conditions. Transparency is the best cure for moral hazard. Most companies are aware of this danger and are interested in minimizing it. Hence, C-level management (which normally comprises the highest-level executives) is the last place to address these issues because strategic ideas require operational effectiveness and efficiency.

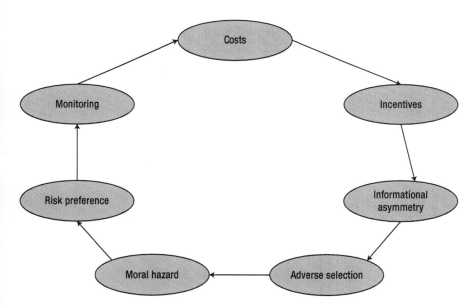

Figure 7-3. *The moral hazard cycle indicates development and consequences of moral hazard. The cycle starts from any change to the system, which opens opportunities and incentives and addresses the basic precondition of asymmetric information between a principal and an agent*

Moral hazard players know how to cover their tracks. Thus, one objective of these companies is to reduce the possibilities of finding and tracing problems. This is often done by finding good alibis and excuses. An indicator that points toward this behavior is a disinclination to use any kind of objective statistics, including data historization or central log files for technical and functional error logging. If transparency exists, development and operations could easily trace any problems or misunderstandings to their causes and hence wouldn't suffer a loss of reputation by delving into trustworthy explanations. A good approach for analyzing root causes for issues is the "five whys" approach, a technique proposed by Taiichi Ohno[12].

Collaborations between development and management are often stable and profitable alliances because the alternative to development is either outlining each conceptual deficit or possibly losing reputation by suddenly being known as a griper (in cases where the overall culture is not open and respectful). Additionally, the extra time consumed for doing all of the work in the project may give rise to conflicting prior expectations such that development becomes spoilsports and even management suffers a loss of reputation. Thus, it is individually rational for all parties to use the circumstances and make their own lives easy. If such behavior is established, returning to normal, constructive work isn't easily possible. Development cannot argue why comparable work will suddenly take longer without the support of management. In turn, management cannot justify increasing costs for equivalent work. However, even if both parties try to end their pointless behavior, other expectations may force the actors to continue to commit moral hazard.

Attributes of a Unified Approach

A unified approach enables development and operations to create concepts collaboratively. A unified approach minimizes conceptual deficits and detects the first stages of these deficits early. By applying the attributes outlined in the sections that follow, concepts can be created in better quality and the pathological actions of participants can be detected.

Foster Traceability

An important aspect of creating conceptional artifacts is that it happens stepwise and may be shared with others with a time delay (i.e., the time between creation and providing to others). Since all concept steps are a solidification of a prior step, all of these aspects are a challenge to the act of creating a good and feasible overall concept. Concept creation is hence a complex, distributed, and iterative process, and deficits can occur on all levels in the concept creation process.

To enable a good understanding, project teams need traceability. It becomes elementary to line up and illustrate the steps as single phases, from the idea to concrete requirements to implementing and operations of software, and also to examine the transitions in between. Such an understanding can be gained, for example, by setting up a value stream mapping, as explained in Chapter 6.

The software solution is a product of a sequence of decisions, thus these decisions should be documented where they have been made ("design rationale"). A prerequisite for traceability is that requirements are well documented. Often the "sensitivity points" approach is used to document requirements.[13] *Software Architecture in Practice*[14] is a great book that delivers further insight about how to handle nonfunctional requirements from an architect's viewpoint.[15] In

---

[12]See Taiichi Ohno, *Toyota Production System: Beyond Large Scale Production* (Productivity Press, 1988), page 17.

[13]See http://www.scribd.com/doc/49571808/14/Sensitivity-and-Tradeoff-Points.

[14]Len Bass et al., *Software Architecture in Practice* (Addison-Wesley, 2009).

[15]Thanks to Prof. Dr. Michael Stal and Stefan Tilkov for providing feedback.

Chapter 4 you learned that scenarios can be used to describe quality attributes. The example in Table 4-1 was taken from the book *Software Architecture in Practice*. Another possible approach for fostering traceability is task-based development, which links work items to other work items.[16] Alistair Cockburn prefers linking nonfunctional requirements to use cases.[17] Associated documents can be written as spreadsheets or in the form of simple tables.

Figure 7-4 illustrates how different artifacts are logically linked (e.g., by a unique identifier, so the identifier of a requirement is included in the software code by using comments in the code) and related to one another to foster traceability. The business case triggers functional and nonfunctional requirements, which in turn results in code and infrastructure (for details how to specify infrastructure, see Chapter 9). They all provide conceptual feedback and improve quality. Linking artifacts helps to trace and avoid conceptual deficits. A graphical representation of a collection of linked artifacts looks similar to a mosaic. The analogy of a mosaic emphasizes the composition and decomposition of conceptual artifacts from one step to the next, from the start of the process (a business case) to the end (having the software in production to deliver a valuable solution to the customer), which ends in a complete picture (specifications, code) of the software (similar to a collection of small mosaics that make up a complete window).

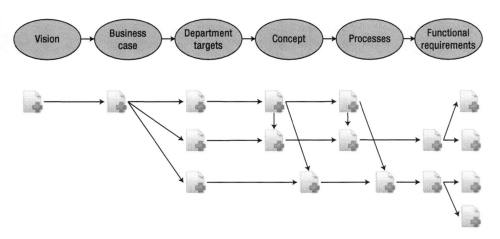

Figure 7-4. *Linked conceptual artifacts provide feedback, foster traceability, and improve quality. Conceptual artifacts, including business cases, functional and nonfunctional requirements, code, and infrastructure specifications, are closely related and are logically linked*

Let's now explore how checked nonfunctional requirements help to drive a unified approach.

---

[16]See Michael Hüttermann, *Agile ALM* (Manning, 2011), Chapter 4.
[17]See Alistair Cockburn, *Writing Effective Use Cases* (Addison-Wesley, 2001), pages 14 and 161.

Check Nonfunctional Requirements

Nonfunctional requirements should be checked. A prerequisite is that the software must be testable.[18] There are many different ways to test nonfunctional requirements, and no silver bullet exists.

It is important to take care of nonfunctional requirements from the beginning of the development process. In most cases it's not possible (or very expensive) to implement nonfunctional requirements post mortem, i.e. after the software is already implemented. That's the reason why DevOps with its close collaboration between development and operations is that important.

Code that fulfills nonfunctional requirements is often clean, simple and testable. If the software is testable, you can write tests for both functional and nonfunctional requirements.[19] For example, Lisa Crispin and Janet Gregory introduce a use case on how to apply test-driven development to check nonfunctional requirements. James Whittaker et al. describe how Google performs load testing as part of the continuous integration solution.[20] Other examples show how to test infrastructure (see Chapter 9 or Tyler Croy's blog post[21]) and use monitoring to manage, evolve, and check nonfunctional requirements (see Chapter 3). In Chapter 10 we'll go through a comprehensive example that shows how to write acceptance tests as executable specifications. The books Continuous Delivery[22] and Release It![23] contain some good advice about checking nonfunctional requirements.

Another approach to check nonfunctional requirements is to link the (nonfunctional) requirement to artifacts where design decisions are made and are documented. A typical example is to logically link the requirement (with its unique identifier) to architecture documents or to software modules.

Align Goals

Sometimes, management is not aligned with the same goals of the company overall, which can result in subversive department behavior or individual activities driven by a hidden agenda. Unfortunately, management defines the requirements and hence can sweep a lot of dirt under the carpet because management also only reports to the C level. Additionally, if there are suspicions, the problem is often declared to be a mere technical problem until it is undeniably proven to be a conceptual deficit of other departments. Conversely, IT authorities usually comprise the smallest proportion of management and hence often fear suffering a loss in reputation by providing evidence too often. This problem exists because the causality between effects and conceptual deficit is not easy to explain to C-level management and cannot be quickly retrieved. Thus, by going into too many arguments without giving immediate and understandable answers, IT authorities often quickly end up in complicated situations. For more information on how to align with goals, see Chapter 5.

---

[18]Frank Buschmann et al. describe testability as a nonfunctional property of software architecture. See their *Pattern-Oriented Software Architecture*, Vol. 1 (Wiley, 1996), page 408.

[19]See Lisa Crispin and Janet Gregory, *Agile Testing* (Addison-Wesley, 2009), page 104.

[20]See James Whittaker et al., *How Google Tests Software* (Addison-Wesley, 2012), page 197.

[21]See http://unethicalblogger.com/2012/06/10/outside-in-to-ops.html.

[22]See Jez Humble and David Farley, *Continuous Delivery* (Addison-Wesley, 2011), Chapter 9.

[23]See Michael T. Nygard, *Release It!* (Pragmatic Bookshelf, 2007).

Creating concepts, particularly writing requirements, is an important area in which the teams of development and operations need to make agreements. Writing requirements documentation is done to guide future actions in developing the solution. "Much of the requirements work will be negated if choices, impositions and assumptions are not both understood and accepted by everyone involved. Thus, before moving out of the requirements phase into the rest of the process, all parties must understand and accept their responsibilities. Otherwise, customers will be disappointed when the product is delivered. To ensure understanding and acceptance, you must attempt to convert every choice, imposition, and assumption into explicit, documented agreements."[24]

Conclusion

This chapter has provided background elaboration on concepts, particularly nonfunctional requirements, and conceptual deficits. Conceptual deficits may have different origins. They may come from limited rationality, complex and dynamic environments, the principal-agent problem, or from moral hazard. You've learned that it's important to minimize conceptual deficits and detect them early. For that reason, traceability, aligned goals, and checks are important. This chapter closes the process view of DevOps. The next part will discuss the technical viewpoint of DevOps.

---

[24]See Donald C. Gause and Gerald M. Weinberg, *Exploring Requirements: Quality Before Design* (Dorset House, 1998), page 274.

Technical View

This final part examines the technical components that comprise DevOps. You'll learn the basics and tools for automating the release process to gain faster feedback.

Automatic Releasing

Survey is show junior devops are still believe in Tooth Fairy, Santa Claus and documentation.

—DevOps Borat[1]

In earlier chapters, you learned about the importance of automation as a vehicle for reducing cycle time and for fostering collaboration between development and operations. In Chapter 3 you learned that automatic releasing is a building block of DevOps and that it can be a powerful strategy to decouple deployment and release.

Automatic releasing reduces the risk of releasing software, ensures repeatability, and, above all, helps to gain fast feedback. Automating error-prone, repetitive, and time-consuming activities is essential.

In this chapter, we'll discuss prerequisites of automatic releasing and explore a few concrete examples and patterns on how to implement automatic releasing. I'll illustrate these examples by discussing common standards and good practices[2] or concrete lightweight tools. First, we need to discuss the prerequisites of automatic releasing.

Prerequisites for Automatic Releasing

From a technical viewpoint, releasing means integrating the work of the team and compiling, linking, packaging, and deploying the software to environments (often also referred to as target systems). The essential parts of releasing are managing the infrastructure, installing the correct version in the infrastructure, and configuring the application according to that specific environment. Releasing is the process of making changes available to the end user. A deployment can result in a release, but that's not mandatory (see Chapter 3). Rollout, deploying, and releasing are

---

[1] http://twitter.com/devops_borat/status/192315498443190272.
[2] Be careful when using the words "standards" and "best practices." Standards and best practices are often context sensitive and dependent on individual requirements.

often used as synonyms to describe activities of this transition phase (see Chapter 1). From a functional viewpoint, releasing means providing a version of the software to the user that implements the customer's requirements. The content of a release is tested and deployed as a single entity.

ENVIRONMENTS AND INFRASTRUCTURE

According to Humble and Farley, an "environment is all of the resources that your application needs to work and their configuration" (*Continuous Delivery* [Addison-Wesley, 2011], page 277), as well as the hardware configuration (including CPUs, memory, and spindles) and the configuration of the operating system and middleware (including messaging systems and web servers). The term infrastructure summarizes all of the environments in your organization together with supporting services, such as firewalls and monitoring systems.

The technical and functional viewpoints should be combined. For example, you should always be able to nail down which requirements are implemented in which software version. Releasing software to a target system is always a synchronization point for the software itself, the infrastructure, and the people. Often, "done" is considered to be exactly that: the point at which the software has been successfully deployed and configured to a target system so that the user can work with it. Under automatic releasing, major parts of the release process are performed by scripts and tool chains. In this process, the whole team profits from automation and, under optimal conditions, simply presses a specific button to promote automatically created release candidates to release status (see Figure 8-1).

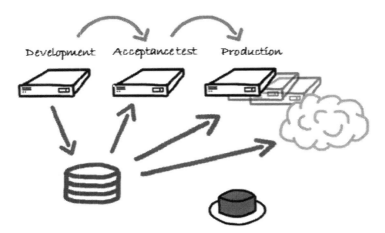

Figure 8-1. *In an automatic releasing process, major parts of the process are accomplished automatically. Often, it's up to the domain expert to decide which release candidate is promoted to release status (e.g., by pressing a specific button).*[3]

---

[3] My thanks to Udo Pracht for the idea of this figure.

Often, this description is an idealistic and oversimplified one (e.g., because of exploratory testing and the need for signing documents before the software can go live in production). However, in all cases, human activities are focused on tasks that only can be performed by humans. To gain fast feedback and synchronize across departments continuously, scripts and tool chains support or completely perform repetitive tasks.

The prerequisites of a holistic automatic releasing process include the following:

- Promote team commitment in collaborative working environments.

- Use highly integrated tool chains consisting of lightweight tools (e.g., Jenkins,[4] Sonar, Maven, and many others) that can be chosen and orchestrated as needed and that are aligned with specific requirements. Individual[5] requirements should be the bases for decisions to choose one tool over the other.

- Put configuration items (including sources, database scripts, middleware, infrastructure, configuration files, such as Java properties files, and build/deploy scripts) into version control.

- Use declarative formats to set up the automation and releasing process, wherever possible (see Chapter 9 for examples).

- Declare (explicitly) and isolate dependencies of application, middleware, and infrastructure.

- Apply continuous integration that continuously synchronizes the work of colleagues, and take special care that you adhere to the following:

  - Don't check in (i.e., commit changes to version control) if the build is broken at that specific time; instead, fix the build immediately.

  - Shape the process (including the definition of done) when you can check in code (e.g., code should compile and tests should run successfully).

  - Fix broken tests; don't comment them out, delete them (unless they are unnecessary) or remove them from the build.

  - Integrate all artifact types, including sources (see the patterns catalog later in this chapter), database scripts (see the patterns catalog later in this chapter), and infrastructure scripts (see Chapter 9).

---

[4] See John Ferguson Smart, *Jenkins: The Definitive Guide* (O'Reilly, 2011).
[5] Typical examples for requirements on tools include the existence of a role base access system, integration options to existing tools, the license model, and many more according to the individual context.

- Distinguish between version control systems (such as Subversion and Git), where you hold your sources, component repositories (such as Artifactory and Nexus), and package repositories (such as YUM, where you hold your software binaries (see the patterns catalog later in this chapter).

- Build binaries once and deploy them to target systems by configuration (i.e., runtime configuration data are not packaged into the binaries in a static fashion; rather, the application is configured during deployment time or upon startup).

- Smoke test deployments to ensure that the deployment went well (see Chapter 3).

- Keep environments similar between development and operations (keeping them equal is not practical because of costs and benefits and different nonfunctional requirements in specific environments).

- Define a process (also for patching and merging back changes in production versions).

- Cover repetitive and time-consuming tasks through automation. Try to automate as much as possible, but remember the costs of and the "paradox" of automation (see Chapter 3).

- Ensure that delivered software is solely built by the build server and is neither built manually nor patched or built on developers' desktops (to ensure reproducibility).

After learning about the prerequisites of automatic releasing, you're now ready to dive into concrete patterns for automatic releasing with appropriate tools.

Patterns with Appropriate Tools

There are many different approaches, processes, and tools to implement automatic releasing. In the following, I'll provide further guidance and concrete examples to show how you can implement your automatic releasing process. The concepts are independent of any specific platforms or languages. To make the concepts clearer, I'll also include examples of concrete tools. Note that other tools in a specific domain that are not mentioned in this chapter are not necessarily worse than the tools I mention here. However, those tools that I mention are state-of-the-art tools that serve as excellent examples and are widely available. Let's start with the concept of the delivery pipeline.

Use Delivery Pipelines

Delivery pipelines (also called build pipelines or staged builds) comprise a set of steps and their interdependencies for delivering software. These steps may include the following:

- Compiling the software.

- Running unit tests.

- Running audits or metrics.

- Packaging and linking the software.

- Deploying the application with all parts of the software version (e.g., database and infrastructure elements).

- Creating backups of the system.

- Configuring the application (during deployment or runtime).

- Migrating and preparing data.

- Smoke testing the application or deployment.

- Automatic acceptance testing (validating whether the solution is doing the right thing, see Chapter 10).

- Manual testing (above all, exploratory testing) that emphasizes the personal experience and responsibilities of the individual testers (e.g., in testing boundary values) to help accomplish test design and test execution simultaneously.

- Promoting the application (approval) that supports the release of a candidate.

- Creating virtual machines, networks, load balancers, monitoring agents, and other infrastructure elements (see Chapter 9).

- Monitoring the application in production.

A pipeline, particularly a delivery pipeline, is a metaphor for the process of delivering software. It indicates that software changes are inputs to the process (the pipeline) at the beginning and are automatically piped through the whole process to the end of the pipeline, which is the production system.

■ **Note**   Delivery pipelines are often also known as staged builds or build pipelines.

From a more technical viewpoint, a pipeline is a way of grouping build jobs and putting them into relation to one another. In other words, pipelines are a way of orchestrating your build process through a series of quality gates, with automated or manually approval processes at specific stages. Thus, these pipelines streamline the delivery process of software toward production.[6]

All code changes (including infrastructure code, see Chapter 9) enter a pipeline into production. The pipeline promotes software and stages artifacts from the development team to the final release in production. You should take special care in linking all artifact types to consistent releases, and you should realize that the "pipeline" is not a "fire-and-forget" tube. Instead,

---

[6] See Jez Humble and David Farley, *Continuous Delivery* (Addison-Wesley, 2011), Chapter 5.

development and operations are connected and integrated, and feedback from the user is streamed back, and in most cases, the solution is (hopefully) more of an integrated lifecycle and something similar to a pipeline, where both ends of the tube are connected with each other.

Example Pipelines

Part of a pipeline can look like the graph illustrated in Figure 8-2. In this example, the continuous build (which starts with the check in of changes in the version control system) tests and deploys development versions of your freshly produced binary artifacts to a component repository (e.g., Nexus) and to a target environment (e.g., deploying a web application to a web container). As an example, consider a Maven-based build system where you want to share new development versions (in Maven these are so called SNAPSHOT versions) of your artifacts with your colleagues. Afterward, the code is inspected by, for example, Sonar.

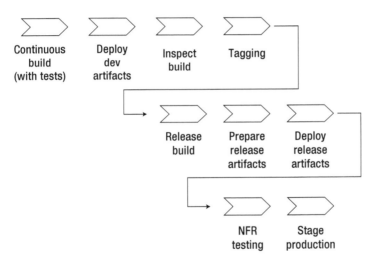

Figure 8-2. *A pipeline that goes through different build steps integrating development and operations. Essentials parts are quality gates (to proceed to another step) and the baseline (tagging the version).*

After verifying that the code satisfies the needs (i.e., the quality gate is passed), you will freeze this specific version in version control (often known as tagging or labeling). In other words, a baseline is created that expresses a release candidate that is a specific version of the software for later reuse. Later, a release build is created. A release build promotes an existing release candidate that will be eligible for production. In our case, the release build is started manually. It prepares release artifacts (in Maven, for example, by removing the SNAPSHOT in version elements) and deploys these artifacts to the component repository. Nonfunctional requirements (NFR) are explicitly tested again before the release is staged to production. Of course, this process is only a small subset of an overall pipeline. In reality, you'll have different further steps that also include deploying the software to additional target systems.

The way you define your pipeline depends on your individual requirements. Let's consider another example that is essentially based on our previous example but that creates the baseline after the release was created and before performing tests on NFR and staging to production (see Figure 8-3).

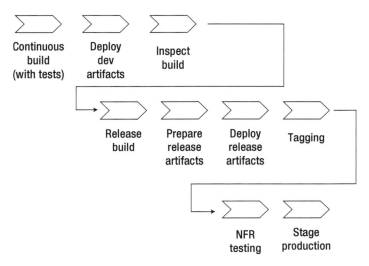

Figure 8-3. *A different example that creates the baseline at the end, after the release artifacts are created. This example is not better or worse than the example in Figure 8-2; it is just different.*

To set up and optimize pipelines, value streams can be used. See Chapter 6 for more information.

Use Baselines

Alexis Leon writes, "A baseline is a specification or product that has been formerly reviewed and agreed on, and serves as a basis for further development."[7] Use baselines that are consistent versions of the software across different artifact types (i.e., all different types of files are included). Baselines can be used again after they've been created. Follow-up work can be put in relation to a baseline (e.g., new change requests or incremental database scripts). A baseline is often a tag (sometimes called a label) in the version control system, which we'll discuss next.

Creating Baselines

From a technical perspective, creating a baseline can be very easy. For example, consider using Subversion as a version control system and Jenkins as the build server. You've configured your

---

[7] See Alexis Leon, *A Guide to Software Configuration Management* (Artech House, 2000), page 354.

Jenkins build job to check out sources and build them. Thus, the Jenkins build job has a workspace with the checked-out sources. After performing other work, the Jenkins build job can simply trigger (e.g., as a shell command):

```
svn cp -m "rel". https://svn.kenai.com/svn/alm~agilealm/scm/tags/$TAG
```

where $TAG is a variable that is used to express the concrete tag. Jenkins will then tag (or copy) the current state of the Jenkins workspace to a new tag in the central Subversion repository.[8] As you can see, adding a Subversion (or Git, CVS, ClearCase) command to Jenkins leaves the domain of Jenkins, and we are using commands of the respective version control tool. For example, we could also trigger something similar to:

```
svn cp -m "Promote"
https://svn.kenai.com/svn/alm~agilealm/scm/tags/$RC
https://svn.kenai.com/svn/alm~agilealm/scm/operations/$RC
```

to copy an existing tag in the Subversion repository to a new tag (e.g., for promoting a release candidate to release status or to hand over a baseline to operations).

Note Don't commit changes back to the baseline. Once created, a baseline does not change over time. Depending on the context, you may want to copy the baseline, change the copy, and create a new baseline from the result, but the original always remains unchanged.

However, it is not always necessary to embed and call scripts to your build job. Often, it is sufficient to use what the build server provides out of the box. Figure 8-4 shows an example of how we use the tagging feature of the Jenkins build job itself to create a tag after the current build job finished successfully.

Perform Subversion tagging on successful build

Tag Base URL	https://svn.kenai.com/svn/alm~agilealm/scm/tags/${env['JOB_NAME']}/v${env['BUILD_ID']}

Figure 8-4. *A different example that creates the baseline at the end, after the release artifacts are created. This example is not better or worse than the script example for tagging explained in the previous text; it is just different.*

---

[8] With Subversion, tags are simply copies of repository paths. This means if you tag an area in your Subversion repository, you copy this area to another place in your Subversion repository.

In this example, we'll again parameterize the build job such that it can create tags dynamically with the relevant parameter. In this case, our tag name consists of the Jenkins build job's name and the unique numeric build identifier for this particular build.

Picking Up Baselines

Once a baseline is created, you can pick it up again any time you want to retrieve the labeled state reproducibly and apply further work on the baseline (e.g., promoting the version or just retrieving the configuration parameters for this specific version). In turn, the additional work that is performed on the defined baseline is again automated, but the trigger that determines which baseline to take is parameterized.

With Jenkins, checking out a baseline is as easy as creating it. For example, one can configure a parameterized build job that expects a string (where you must enter a switch to the relevant baseline) or offers a list of existing Subversion tags. Figure 8-5 shows an example of the latter, where Jenkins passes its variable RC (stands for release candidate) along to further steps in the build job after the user has picked a specific tag. Configuring Jenkins to sort the list based on the newest baselines will result in a list where the user sees the recently created baselines first.

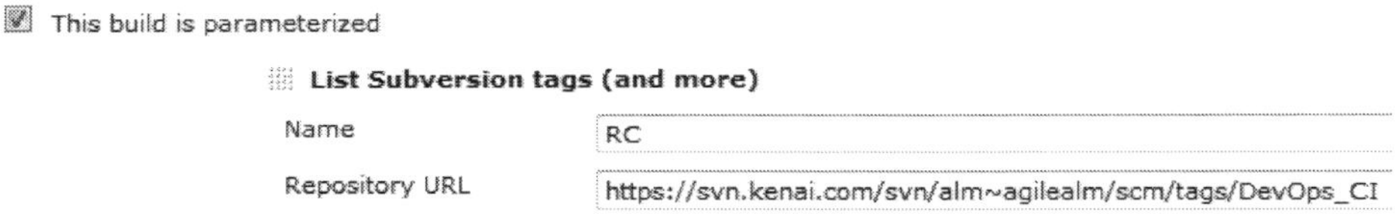

Figure 8-5. *Configuring a parameterized Jenkins build job that will offer a combo box of existing Subversion tags under the defined path. The concrete one (in our case, expressed by the variable RC) is available in the Jenkins build job afterward for further processing.*

We can then combine the baseline with further processing. In a typical example, you configure Jenkins to check out exactly that baseline before applying further actions on it. To this end, we simply have to define the check-out Subversion repository URL, including the parameter (our switch named "RC") that we introduced in the preceding step (see Figure 8-6).

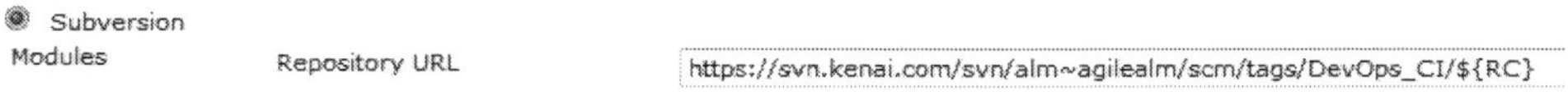

Figure 8-6. *Configuring Jenkins to check out the baseline that is defined by the user on runtime.*

If the Jenkins build is then triggered, the user must perform an input (unless Jenkins is configured to automatically inject parameters from upstream jobs). This is shown in Figure 8-7.

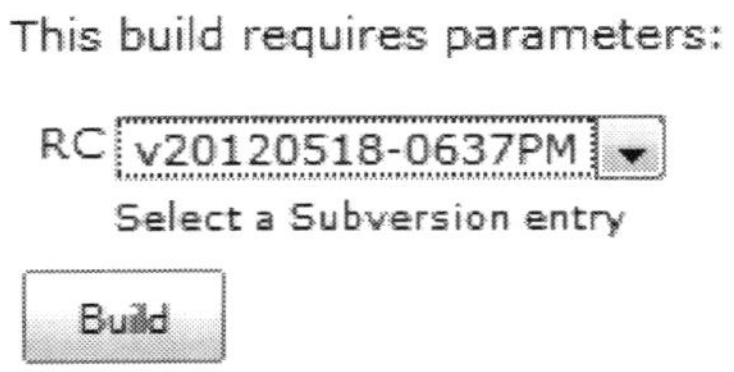

This build requires parameters:

RC `v20120518-0637PM` ▼
Select a Subversion entry

Build

Figure 8-7. *The user must perform an input while starting the build job. The user must choose a tag from a combo box.*

In one easy use case for performing further actions on the baseline, one could package the sources with the build tool Gradle[9] (see Listing 8-1).

Listing 8-1. *Packing Code from a Baseline*

```
apply plugin: 'java'

import java.io.BufferedReader;
import java.io.FileNotFoundException;
import java.io.FileReader;
import java.io.IOException;

task zip(type: Zip) {
    BufferedReader bufferedReader = null;
    bufferedReader = new BufferedReader(new FileReader('version'));
    String version;
    version = bufferedReader.readLine();
    from('component') {
        include '**/*'
        into('software-'+version+'/component')
    }
    baseName = 'software-'+version;
}
```

In this example, a file called "version" is located in the root path. The file contains a version number of the application (that was injected during build time). The version number will be part of the package name (i.e. the name of the file in Zip file format).

After discussing baselines, we can now discuss shared version numbers, which is another way to integrate development and operations.

---

[9] See http://www.gradle.org.

Shared Version Numbers

Have you ever experienced a version number zoo where developers, operations, and businesses all used their own version numbers to express the exact same software version? With DevOps, it is essential to find shared names for versions across departments. As already discussed, collaboratively sharing a version control system (such as Subversion) will foster collaboration between development and operations. So why not use and share version numbers that are derived from the version control system? In our example, while using Subversion, the Subversion revision number can serve as a communication vehicle or even a version number can do so. This approach has many advantages:

- The Subversion revision number is unique (for one Subversion repository).

- The Subversion revision number is autoincremented by Subversion itself. Thus, there is no need for one's own error-prone scripts.

- The Subversion revision number is stable. For example, using a Jenkins build job name is not stable because it can be renamed easily. A Jenkins job number is not stable because it is not unique.

Let's now explore how to access revision numbers from Subversion.

Accessing Revision Numbers

Is it difficult to access a revision number out of Jenkins? No, definitely not. In one easy scenario, we could use Jenkins's postbuild Groovy plug-in.[10] With the help of this plug-in, we can code a Groovy code that is executed as part of the Jenkins build. As Listing 8-2 shows, we take the aforementioned variable RC to access the baseline.

Listing 8-2. *Accessing and Propagating a Revision Number According to a Defined Baseline*

```
ver = manager.build.buildVariables.get("RC")
manager.createSummary("gear2.gif").appendText(ver, false)
if(manager.build.result.isBetterOrEqualTo(hudson.model.Result.UNSTABLE)) {
    def cmd = "svn log
https://svn.kenai.com/svn/alm~agilealm/scm/tags/DevOps_CI/$ver-v --stop-on-
copy -limit 1"
    def txt = cmd.execute().text
    def strippedTxt = (txt = ~ /--/).replaceAll("")
    def rev = strippedTxt.tokenize('|')[0].trim()
    manager.addShortText(rev)
}
```

We then display the baseline as part of our Jenkins build result page (via the `manager.createSummary` process). Afterward, we define a native Subversion command. The command

---

[10] See https://wiki.jenkins-ci.org/display/JENKINS/Groovy+Postbuild+Plugin.

pulls log information from Subversion according to the baseline. We simply take the first log entry and strip and pull out the revision number. The '-r 1:HEAD' reverses the order of the log to return the entries from oldest to newest. The flags --stop-on-copy and --limit 1 precisely deliver the oldest log entry on that tag (which is the copy operation itself), regardless of whether the tag has been changed after creation (thus becoming a branch by definition).

After we've retrieved the revision number, let's now pass it through the system and make it visible.

Passing Revision Numbers

After parsing, the variable rev will then contain the Subversion revision number that belongs to the existing tag. We can do many things with the revision number, including adding the number to the names of artifacts or adding a short text to the Jenkins build information. As Figure 8-8 shows, the concrete job that was parameterized and run on a baseline is labeled with the revision number as well.

Figure 8-8. *In Jenkins, the build job history is labeled with the Subversion revision number.*

Propagating and sharing versions appropriately is essential. However, the process by which artifacts are technically labeled can be a bit tricky, as shown in the next section.

Version Automatically

Setting version numbers automatically is often a pain point in the automatic releasing process. The first advice you should follow is to apply what the tools offer. Let's consider a small example that is based on Maven, the leading build tool for Java projects. The build tool is famous for its dependency management (i.e., its capacity to define and automatically resolve dependencies during build time) and its ability to distinguish between SNAPSHOT development versions (which contain the SNAPSHOT token in the version element) and release artifacts (which contain only a plain version in the version element without -SNAPSHOT). With Maven, you must assign so-called coordinates to a project (which will produce a binary). An easy example is shown as follows:

```
<groupId>com.huettermann</groupId>
<artifactId>devops</artifactId>
<version>1.0.13-SNAPSHOT</version>
<name>DevOps</name>
```

At a specific moment in time, you'll want to promote development versions (in our small example, it is 1.0.13-SNAPSHOT) to release versions (which would be 1.0.13). Comprehensive solutions exist, such as the Maven release plug-in or Jenkins/Artifactory[11] staging facility, but in special situations, they may not be the best solution to implement your individual requirements. In that case, you may prefer a lightweight approach, which we'll explore next.

Parameterizing Maven's Versions Plug-In

To release artifacts with Maven, you can simply use the Maven version's plug-in.[12] Its goal (named "set") sets the current project's version and also updates all versions of child modules. Thus, the command used is a straight versions:set -DnewVersion=1.0.0 (with appropriate parameters) that has to be performed on a Maven project. In this example, it sets the Maven version to 1.0.0.

However, what can you do if your Maven POM's[13] *version* element is the only place where you've stored the version number (compared to storing it in a central place separately; one example of that is shown in Listing 8-1)? For example, to release a version 1.0.0-SNAPSHOT to version 1.0.0, you need to know which current version to look for (unless you script another smart solution to strip the snapshot token). Let's write our own easy Maven plug-in that looks similar to the plug-in shown in Listing 8-3.

Listing 8-3. *A simple Maven plug-in that takes the current version (which is a SNAPSHOT version), strips the SNAPSHOT token, and returns the new version as a property that can be evaluated by further build steps.*

```
package com.huettermann;
import org.apache.maven.plugin.AbstractMojo;
import org.apache.maven.plugin.MojoExecutionException;
import org.apache.maven.project.MavenProject;

/**
 * @goal release
 * @phase process-sources
 */
public class ReleaseMojo extends AbstractMojo {
    /**
     * @parameter expression="${project}"
     * @readonly
     */
    Private MavenProject project;
    public void execute() throws MojoExecutionException {

        String version=project.getVersion();
        String release=version;
```

---

[11] See http://maven.apache.org/plugins/maven-release-plugin/ or https://wiki.jenkins-ci.org/display/JENKINS/Jenkins+Artifactory+Plugin+-+Release+Management.

[12] See http://mojo.codehaus.org/versions-maven-plugin/.

[13] With Maven, build information is stored in the project object model (POM). For more information about Maven in general, and POMs in particular, see the free online book at www.sonatype.com/book/.

```
    if (version.indexOf("-SNAPSHOT") > -1) {
        release = version.substring(0, version.indexOf("-SNAPSHOT"));
        getLog().info("SNAPSHOT found: " + release);
    }
    project.getProperties().setProperty("newVersion", release);
  }
}
```

The Maven plug-in needs a POM that also defines the coordinates of the plug-in[14] (i.e., the identifier to use the plug-in later in the process). In our example, the coordinates are:

```
<groupId > com.huettermann</groupId>
<artifactId > release</artifactId>
<version > 1.0-SNAPSHOT</version>
```

We can call the plug-in by using a concatenation of the values of these coordinates and adding the defined entry point to the plug-in (that is what we defined with the @goal annotation in Listing 8-3). The resulting string for the call looks like this:

```
com.huettermann:release:1.0-SNAPSHOT:release
```

We utilize our plug-in by adding the call into Jenkins, where it is called during build time, which we'll explore next.

Calling During Build Time

The Maven plug-in scans the version of the current Maven project and strips off the -SNAPSHOT suffix to derive the release version. The new version is then set as a property that can be accessed by further build steps. Figure 8-9 shows the results of embedding this plug-in as a build step in our Jenkins build[15].

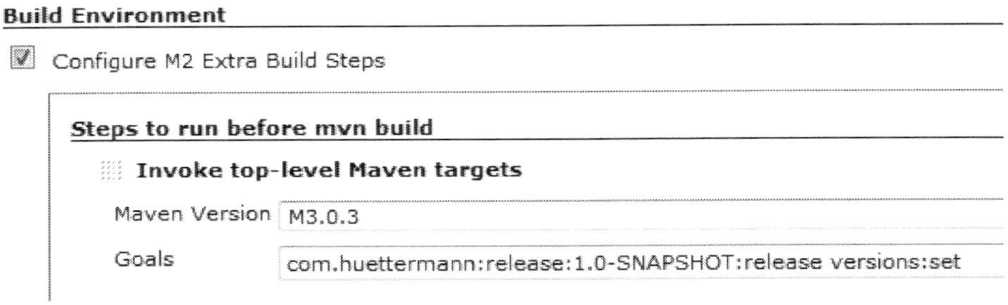

Build Environment

☑ Configure M2 Extra Build Steps

> **Steps to run before mvn build**
>
> ▦ **Invoke top-level Maven targets**
>
> Maven Version `M3.0.3`
>
> Goals `com.huettermann:release:1.0-SNAPSHOT:release versions:set`

Figure 8-9. *Calling the Maven plug-in that returns the new version number. In turn, the returned version number is an input for the* versions:set *call.*

---

[14] For more information on Maven plug-ins, see
http://maven.apache.org/guides/plugin/guide-java-plugin-development.html.

[15] Adding other steps can be helpful too, for example adding a check whether SNAPSHOT dependencies are still used during releasing. Those checks can be performed with the maven-enforcer-plugin, see http://maven.apache.org/plugins/maven-enforcer-plugin.

The property newVersion was set by the Maven plug-in, and its name maps to the input parameter of Maven's versions:set goal.

If you already have the version number (e.g., the version number is injected into a parameterized build by a string parameter), then it is even easier to call the Maven goal (see Figure 8.10). This time, we add the parameter –DgenerateBackupPoms and set it to false to suppress the creation of backup files.

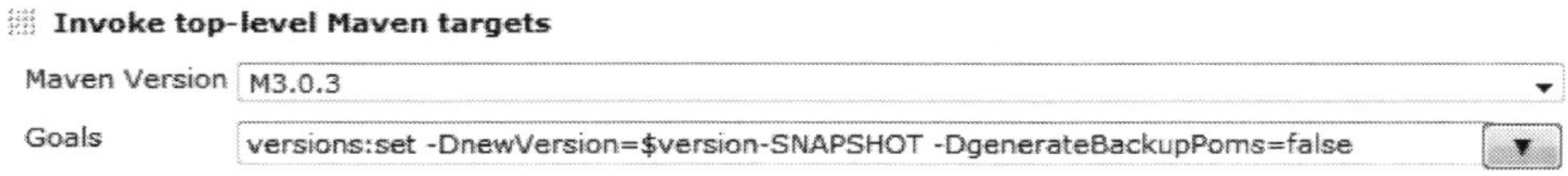

▦ **Invoke top-level Maven targets**

Maven Version	M3.0.3	▾
Goals	versions:set -DnewVersion=$version-SNAPSHOT -DgenerateBackupPoms=false	▾

Figure 8-10. *Calling* versions:set, *where the new version is available already during build time.*

Further Approaches

This solution can also simply set the new development version after a release is built, and the code of the project must be aligned with the new development version.

There are many other possible solutions as well. For example, you can fire a shell script as part of your Jenkins build that replaces version numbers accordingly in your Jenkins workspace.

After preparing the new version (i.e., changing the code), you can check in the change. This can also be achieved by a shell command in Jenkins:

```
svn commit -m "new development version"
```

After discussing numerous tips and tricks for handling baselines, we now take a look at forming release containers with RPM (RedHat Package Manager).

Use Release Containers with RPM

Using standards and tools that are native to the used platform can be a very good idea when setting up a holistic software delivery process. With the following example, I'll illustrate how to use RPMs as a container for your software and to configure the installed (or updated) application during installation time.

Overview of Topology

As a part of a continuous build, a build server (e.g., Jenkins) checks out sources and builds scripts from a version control system (see Figure 8-11).

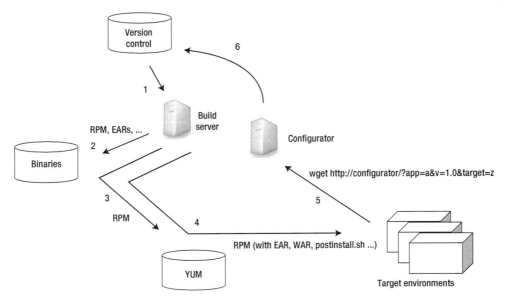

Figure 8-11. *An example of a development or delivery process for Linux-based target systems using RPMs as the container for the software. Software is configured during the installation process.*

The build server builds the software and deploys produced binaries into a component repository (also called a binary repository). A specific release build aggregates all relevant software elements and packages an RPM file.

■ **Note** RPMs provide a powerful mechanism to form release containers. Without using release containers, it is not always clear which ingredients or changes are part of a release, and, in practice, finding missing parts is often an activity similar to finding needles in a haystack. In order to put infrastructure elements into a release container, tools such as Puppet can be used too, and RPMs and Puppet are often used in conjunction. Puppet can also be used to distribute RPMs to target machines. We'll discuss Puppet in Chapter 9.

The RPM file is a release container that contains all relevant facets of the software, including a specific version of a new standard software package on the target system or produced artifacts (e.g., a standard Java deployment unit, such as an enterprise archive [EAR]). RPM is a free software packaging manager that contains the package format itself (files have the extension .rpm) and all necessary software tools to create and manage software RPM packages. The core of the logic used to create an RPM is a "spec" file, the specification of an RPM.

RPM Spec File and Configuration

Spec files contain the package name, the version, and the steps to build, install, and clean a package. An example RPM file can look like the one shown in Listing 8-4.

Listing 8-4. *An Example RPM that Includes an EAR File as a Source for Distribution. The percent sign marks different sections in the spec file. The postinstall section includes a reference to a postinstall configuration script.*

```
%define name myname
%define release 1
%define version 1.0.0
Summary: A wonderful program.
Name: %{name}
Version: %{version}
Release: %{release}
Source0: SOURCES/%{name}.ear
%prep
%build
%files
.. %{name}.ear
%install
%post
/../configure.sh
```

RPM packages are created from a spec file by using the rpmbuild tool.[16]

In our example, the release build (triggered by the build server) copies the RPM file to a YUM software repository. YUM[17] is a free software package manager that installs, updates, and removes packages on RPM-based systems. As a part of YUM's services, it manages dependencies automatically and serves as a convenient approach to manage and distribute individual RPMs. YUM is implemented as a local file directory.

If the RPM-based software is installed on a Linux-based target environment, it scans all configured software repositories to retrieve the RPM in its desired version, downloads it to the target environment, and installs it. Complementary tools such as YaST[18] are useful for installing and configuring software. In our scenario, the RPM distributes the environment-agnostic artifacts. That is, the RPM can be reused in all environments and does not contain configuration information that is specific to a concrete target environment. As part of the RPM, a postinstall script can be bundled and called during the installation process. The postinstall script can contain a call to a web service (the "configurator"), for example, by calling a wget. The configurator serves as a facade to standardize and reuse packages and to specialize accordingly.

The wget contains parameters such as the application and version to be installed and the concrete target environment. The configurator contacts the configuration pool (which holds all configuration data that are specific to environments) and returns the needed correct

---

[16] For more information about RPM, see http://www.rpm.org.

[17] http://fedoraproject.org/wiki/Yum.

[18] YaST (Yet another Setup Tool) is an RPM-based setup and configuration tool, see http://en.opensuse.org/Portal:YaST.

configuration data. In our case, the configuration pool is the version control system, but other implementation options are possible, such as the binary manager or a database (such as a configuration management database [CMDB]). The only precondition is that the configuration data are a versioned part of the software (respectively, its baseline) and can be retrieved reproducibly.

The environment-specific configuration data are returned to the caller (e.g., as a Zip file) and are placed on the target system as part of the installation or its configuration. This approach is also very useful for developers to use on their desktops. For example, using Maven profiles enables a light local installation to be configured as well. The final push to install the software on a target environment is either performed manually, triggered by the build server, or conducted by an appropriate tool (e.g., Puppet; see Chapter 9).

Apply Task-Based Development

Unfortunately, development and operations too often use distinct processes and tools, which results in silos. In this section, we cover how we can align processes with tasks and shared tools, for example with:

- JIRA (a bug tracker and planner, see `http://atlassian.com/jira`) for incident management.

- Artifactory (a binary manager, see `http://www.jfrog.com/products.php`) for artifact exchange between development and operations.

Work items (issues, defects, incidents) should be managed with a defect-tracking tool, such as JIRA. DevOps means that both development and operations use the same ticket system to track and synchronize their work. However, the tools are only one aspect. What about the process? DevOps can be implemented by using common units of work that are shared across teams. One possible solution uses "tasks."

Tasks are spread across artifact types, project phases, and tools. A task can be any one of the following: a fine-grained, measurable unit of work; a change; an incident in production or sliced from a broader scope, such as a use case; or simply an incident in production. With a task-based approach, the task is the unit of interaction for all participants, especially developers and operations. A task can serve as a perfect exchange vehicle for implementing DevOps.

Prerequisites and Context

In Chapter 7 you learned the basics of task-based development as an approach for maintaining conceptual integrity. Task-based development comprises the linking of work items (issues, defects) to a specific set of changes (such as an atomic change set) made to complete the work described in the work item. For example, if you're fixing a defect that's listed as defect 55 in JIRA, task-based development requires that you link the exact set of changes to defect 55 in JIRA. The used tools then make the information about the task and its change set available. For more information about task-based development, see Chapter 4 of "Agile ALM"[19].

---

[19] Michael Hüttermann, *Agile ALM*, (Manning, 2011).

Every check in to version control leads to a potential release. However, the check in aligns releases with functional work (e.g., a user story is fully implemented and a corresponding ticket in the bug tracker is closed), not technical work (i.e., a developer checks in to version control, but the check in does not lead to a complete and consistent feature). Another reason to align releases with functional work (and not with single commits) is the way you typically address production incidents. Often multiple commits are required to locate (e.g., add additional logging) and fix a bug. In other words, a code change may result in a release and may start the whole process again.

Example with Artifactory

Artifactory is a binary manager that can be smartly integrated with your build server. The features of Artifactory include the following[20]:

- It serves as a tool for artifact exchange and provisioning across all artifact types, including Java, C++, and others.

- It offers support for provisioning RPMs so that it can act as a full-fledged YUM repository.[21]

- It offers support for automatic dependency generation and publishing, not only limited to standard build tools (e.g., Maven and Gradle), but also for generic builds (e.g., deploying dynamic link library [DLL] files).

- It offers tight integration with the build server, such as Jenkins, TeamCity, and Bamboo.

- It promotes already released software versions to other logical repositories by triggering from inside the build server (without the need to rebuild the software).

- It provides full traceability of builds to their produced artifacts.

- It offers role-based access control; tools are used by all, with different permissions on specific operations.

- It provides information about which tasks were addressed in a specific build (task-based development).

- It offers support for replication from build machines to data centers.[22]

As part of the Artifactory integration in build servers, JIRA ticket information is now transported from your build server (e.g., Jenkins) to Artifactory. Once you've installed Jenkins and Artifactory Pro on your system and you've installed the JIRA plug-in for Jenkins and the Jenkins Artifactory plug-in, you are up and running.

---

[20] Thanks to Yoav Landman for giving me feedback.
[21] See http://wiki.jfrog.org/confluence/display/RTF/YUM+Repositories.
[22] See http://wiki.jfrog.org/confluence/display/RTF/Repository+Replication.

The example Build #41 was triggered by a continuous build and references two JIRA tickets (see Figure 8-12).

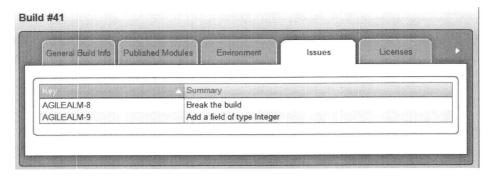

Build #41

Key	Summary
AGILEALM-8	Break the build
AGILEALM-9	Add a field of type Integer

Figure 8-12. *Artifactory shows on which tickets the teams worked on (in our case two) in the context of a specific build (in our case #41).*

Afterward, we start a release build (which releases the Maven artifacts) and a promotion build (which promotes the produced artifacts to a different staging repository). This build is #42 (which, conveniently, appears to be the answer to everything), and the release history is documented Artifactory's release history panel.

Now let's look at a final pattern for automatic releasing. We'll discover how to handle database changes automatically.

Use Database Update Scripts

With DevOps, database elements should also be released automatically. It is a good idea to distinguish between database *expansion scripts* and *contraction scripts.*[23] Expansion scripts are database changes that can be applied without breaking the database's backward compatibility with the existing version of the application (e.g., adding elements such as new tables or columns). These scripts can run at any point before upgrading the corresponding application. Contraction scripts migrate the database and break backward compatibility (e.g., removing structure or cleaning up). This process conveniently decouples database migrations from application deployments.

Releasing Automatically

One of the more advanced challenges in automatically releasing databases is to link the database in its current version (i.e., the current set of structural elements such as tables and columns, and their data), or, in other words, in its current state, with the current version of the rest

---

[23] See http://exortech.com/blog/2009/02/01/weekly-release-blog-11-zero-downtime-database-deployment/.

of what makes up the complete release. By having database elements in version control already, you can create tags and add all of your configuration items to a defined baseline.

Automatically deploying database changes results in the need for a process that supports applying database changes incrementally while preserving current structure and content. Many approaches exist for updating an existing database, and all have the following activities in common:

1. Put all database elements (and all change sets) to version control.

2. Create SQL (structured query language) scripts that have to be applied to roll forward to the next version and to roll backward to the previous version of the database. These scripts are grouped into single change sets.

3. Create one file for each change set, to hold the respective change set. Change sets move the database forward (or backward). Change sets are applied based on a baseline. Thus the concrete content of a change set may contradict a previous change set.

4. Create baselines where you freeze all configuration items of your application, including the database elements.

5. Retrieve the baseline for deployment:

   a. In cases of a full installation, apply again all available database elements and change sets.

   b. In cases of incremental installation, check the current state (the version) of the specific database and apply all new change sets to it (that have not been applied before).

How and where can you store the existing database state? One approach is to use a database table column that holds the version of the database scheme. Additionally, you can create columns for SQL scripts that have to be applied to roll forward and to roll backward. Shell scripts can now roll backward or forward using the information held in the database.

Example for Handling Change Sets

Let's go through a simple example that illustrates the common concepts of how you can handle and apply change sets to your database. First, we need a folder that contains the database change sets. This folder is also put to version control. For change sets, the following rules apply:

- Each change set can consist of multiple SQL statements.

- Each change set is stored in a separate file.

- Each change set is named uniquely by naming the file uniquely.

To make it clearer, an example change set could be:

```
ALTER TABLE cars RENAME TO bikes;
```

And we store the change set in the file changeset47.sql, because we've already created 46 change sets before this one. Another example change set could be:

```
ALTER TABLE bikes ADD color varchar2(50);
```

And we store it in file changeset93.sql. Before the team starts with change sets, it's important to agree on a naming pattern for the files. All change set files have the same name except the number (that is part of the name) that is incremented per change set.

Our deployment process picks up a baseline from version control. The database change sets are placed into a working directory. We can now start a shell script that could look like the one given in Listing 8-5.

Listing 8-5. *A Shell Script Iterates Over All Change Sets and Applies Change Sets that Haven't Been Installed Yet*

```
flag = 0
if [ -f lastRun.txt ]; then
    pastRun = `cat lastRun.txt`
else pastRun = 0
fi

next = `expr $pastRun + 1`
startWithScript = ch$next.sql

for x in `ls *.sql`; do
    if [ "$startWithScript" == $x ]; then
        flag = 1
    fi
    if [ "$flag" == 1 ]; then
        echo $x | egrep "[0-9]{1,}" -o  > lastRun.txt
        #execute the file here with your database client
    fi
done
```

The script creates the version file named lastRun.txt if it wasn't created before. The script stores the current version number in a variable pastRun and constructs the name pattern that the next change set file must match. The rest is more simple common shell scripting. We'll iterate this through the directory of change sets that is ordered by name. If we've found the next change set (according to the file matcher we've computed before), we'll apply this and all further available change sets. We strip the version number from the file name and store it in the file lastRun.txt. In every iteration of your loop through all change sets, this file will be replaced and always contains the number of the currently processed change set. As part of the loop, we need to execute the change set. All change set files are valid SQL scripts, thus we just need to use our respective database client and apply the file. That's it.

■ **Note**   Please keep in mind that the example in this section is simplified. For example, to store the version of the database in a flat file is a pragmatic approach. In many situations you will store the version information in a dedicated table in the database itself. Additionally, you will probably add logging as well as *commit* and *rollback* routines.

To make this example easy, we've placed all these files, the change sets, and the version number file (i.e., the value of lastrun.txt) into one folder. In practice, you should place the version number in another location on your server. Similarly, access restrictions, transaction handling, and further ramp up codes (such as connecting to the database or setting up a path for the database client) were not part of this example.

Backward roll can be based on a shell script that just iterates through the directory by reverse order, for example:

```
for x in `ls *.sql | sort -r`; do
    #do processing here
done
```

Tools like Liquibase and Flyway[24] are based on the concepts introduced in this section.

Conclusion

This chapter explored automatic releasing. I described the intentions and prerequisites of automatic releasing and offered some concrete examples on how to release automatically. Please keep in mind that some steps in the automated process are often still performed manually. One typical example is the process that decides which release candidate is promoted to release status. Automation is not performed for its own sake. Rather, automation is supposed to deliver fast feedback about all different stakeholders and synchronize both stakeholders and the software. The next chapter covers infrastructure as code, which emphasizes that your automatic release process should include all of the different artifacts of your release. That is, the process should include not only the software itself but also infrastructure information.

---

[24] http://www.liquibase.org/ and Flyway http://code.google.com/p/flyway.

Infrastructure as Code

To make error is human. To propagate error to all server in automatic way is #devops.

—DevOps Borat[1]

Recent years have seen the rise of disciplines like continuous integration, test driven development, build/deployment automation, and more. All of these had a purpose to automate as many parts as possible of the lifecycle of a software product. However, the main focus often is the software itself, and the infrastructure on which the software runs is still quite often a "work of art."

In a classic sense, infrastructure summarizes items such as operating systems, servers, switches, and routers (see Chapter3). According to other definitions, infrastructure comprises all of the environments of an organization together with supporting services, such as firewalls and monitoring services (see Chapter 8). The use of the term *infrastructure as code* is widespread these days. In this context, infrastructure is often thought to include every part of the solution that is not the developed software application itself (although even the software is included occasionally). In that sense, infrastructure is meant to include the middleware (such as web servers with configuration files, software packages as part of the operating system, crontabs, technical users, and so on).

Infrastructure is set up and changed over time, before the software even goes into production. If you're lucky, infrastructure is documented well, but often enough it would not be an easy task to rebuild your infrastructure from scratch if the need would arise.

"Perl was designed as a programming language for automating system administration. It didn't take long for leading-edge sysadmins to realize that handcrafted configurations and nonreproducible incantations were a bad way to run their shops."[2]

---

[1] http://twitter.com/#!/devops_borat/status/41587168870797312.
[2] See Mike Loukides, *What Is DevOps?* (O'Reilly, 2012),
http://radar.oreilly.com/2012/06/what-is-devops.html.

Infrastructure as code has lately become popular to emphasize the need to handle the set up of your infrastructure in the same way you would handle development of your code: pick the right language or tool to do the job and start developing a solution that suits your needs, making it an executable specification that can be applied to target systems efficiently and repeatedly.

This chapter introduces the tools Vagrant,[3] a tool for managing virtualized development environments, and Puppet,[4] a tool for managing infrastructure items that are often also called configurations. Afterward, we'll explore a real-world use that is based on how the development of the build server Jenkins is streamlined by Vagrant and Puppet.

Starting with Infrastructure as Code

Setup and maintenance of infrastructure were automated even before the rise of Agile software development and the DevOps movement. But there have often been handcrafted, scripted solutions, barely readable by someone other than the original author. In recent years, a few tools in the field of configuration management started to gain popularity to address these challenges. These tools help developers and operations to work together and enable more transparency on the infrastructure level. After all, in today's world of ever more complex and distributed IT systems, there's an increasing need for developers to know about operational things and vice versa. The infrastructure as code paradigm and its related tools can help to achieve this goal.

Before we get into more detail, there are two key questions to be addressed:

- Why should I adopt infrastructure as code?

- How should I do it? (which tools can I use?)

To answer these questions, let's first think about the process involved in infrastructure set up when a typical web application gets developed.

Traditional Infrastructure Handling

In the first phase, as the architecture is not yet fixed, developers will try components, eventually ending up in a first draft of the setup. Now, each developer has set up his or her local development environment, with all the components running on the machine. At this point there might not even be a shared environment on which the software gets deployed continuously. That would be the next step. Depending on the organization's structure, this might already be the borderline where the developers are not allowed full access to the target machines anymore and they have to provide the operations team with some sort of assistance on how to get things up. The same might happen again for QA, staging, and production environments. And as reality goes, at least the configuration of the components might change continuously along the way, if not new components being added to the infrastructure.

---

[3] http://vagrantup.com.
[4] http://puppetlabs.com.

Each time developers try things on their local or test environments, they'll then report the change in infrastructure to operations, who then adjust the other environments. You might say this is nonsense if you are working in a startup or a young and small company. But unfortunately this is often the hard reality in larger corporations and, obviously, there is a lot of potential for errors and misunderstandings. Both options, no documentation and documenting infrastructure in Office documents, are suboptimal.

Furthermore the same problems can arise if new developers are added to the team. If the setup is not fully documented or someone made an effort to write a script to at least do parts of the set up, or it is documented but outdated, the new developer might struggle to get everything running smoothly, and finding the error can be a search for the needle in the haystack. There is no central, versionized version of the infrastructure that can be considered to be always runable.

How to Do It Better

Now, let's think about what would be better for everyone involved. Assume that new developers don't have to set up things by hand or partly aided by some scripts (not to mention the potential that the script might not be suitable for the developers operating system or the fact that the developer already has other stuff running his or her machine, which can interfere with the project setup), but can have them writing executable specifications, utilizing virtualization to create and destroy their test environments on the fly, as needed.

Getting new developers on board would simply be a matter of having them check out the specification from the version control repository, execute it, and use the same environment as their colleagues. If the team decides that changes to the infrastructure have reached a stable level, the specification can be used to update any shared environments (e.g., for acceptance or integration tests) and can be passed over to the operations team, who can reuse the specification for staging and production environments. Sounds great, doesn't it?

Well, within the past few years, a number of tools have emerged that address exactly these problems. Some tools existed before terms such as DevOps and infrastructure as code were coined, but these movements helped to further spread the use of these tools and grow the whole community around it.

In this chapter, I'm going to introduce two tools: Vagrant and Puppet. Vagrant allows you to easily build lightweight and portable virtual environments, based on a simple textual description. Puppet is a configuration management tool that uses a declarative syntax to describe the desired state of a target environment and allows this description to be executed to create that state on a target machine. In combination, this can lead to a target topology, similar to that shown in Figure 9-1.

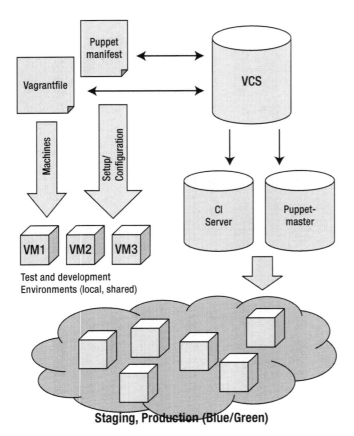

Figure 9-1. *An example topology for infrastructure as code consisting of Vagrant and Puppet artifacts that are stored in a version control system, built continuously with a continuous integration (CI) server.*

In the middle of the solution, Vagrant is used to set up test and development environments (as virtual machines). Puppet is used to provision infrastructure.

Configuration files for both Vagrant and Puppet are versionized in a version control system, with all its benefits, including change control and sharing changes in the whole team. A continuous integration (CI) server, such as Jenkins, listens to changes in version control and could propagate new versions to target environments for test purposes, automatically. Sounds like magic? It is, but don't let it scare you. We'll examine this in much more detail in this chapter. Now let's start with test environments with Vagrant.

Test Environments with Vagrant

Vagrant allows you to build virtual environments in an easy way, based on a textual specification in the so-called Vagrant file. This file is all that is needed to create a virtual environment from scratch.

VIRTUAL ENVIRONMENT

The term *virtual environment* describes a means of delivering computing resources that are independent from physical machines. A virtual environment can enable the running of virtual desktops, servers, or other virtual appliances. The advantage of a virtual environment is that it can more efficiently utilize physical resources while avoiding costly overprovisioning.

Vagrant is based on Ruby[5] and uses Oracles VirtualBox[6] to run virtual machines, so you'll need these before going on with the installation. The easiest way is then to install Vagrant via RubyGems:

```
> sudo gem install vagrant
```

If everything went well, you should see output similar to this:

```
Fetching: vagrant-1.0.2.gem (100%)
Successfully installed vagrant-1.0.2
1 gem installed
Installing ri documentation for vagrant-1.0.2...
Installing RDoc documentation for vagrant-1.0.2...
```

Now you can go on and set up your very first Vagrant environment:

```
> mkdir -p vagrant/test
> cd vagrant/test
> vagrant box add lucid32 http://files.vagrantup.com/lucid32.box
> vagrant init lucid32
```

The Add command will download a Vagrant base box from the given location. Add it to the system under the given alias and store it in $HOME/.vagrant. Base boxes are Vagrant's initial building blocks to create virtual environments. To make life simple here, we stick with the Ubuntu 10.4 box that is offered by the Vagrant team. The second command creates the Vagrant

---

[5] http://www.ruby-lang.org/en.
[6] https://www.virtualbox.org.

file in the current directory. This initial Vagrant file contains a lot of documentation on several options available, so it's worth taking a look at it. The first lines should look like those shown in Listing 9-1.

Listing 9-1. *An Initial Vagrant File*

```
# Every Vagrant virtual environment requires a box to build
config.vm.box = "lucid32"
# The url from where the 'config.vm.box' box will be
# fetched if it doesn't already exist on the user's system.
# config.vm.box_url = "http://domain.com/path/to/above.box"
End
```

The only uncommented option is the name of the base box to build the environment from. This is the Ubuntu box we just added to the system. You can see that there is also the possibility to add a URL to specify where the base box can be downloaded from. Especially if you think you will use Vagrant in a team, this is an important option to make your Vagrant files portable. If the Vagrant file gets used by someone who doesn't have the base box on his or her system already, Vagrant will download it.

A VAGRANT BOX

A "box" is the base image used to create a virtual environment with Vagrant. It is a portable file that can be used by others on any platform that Vagrant runs in order to bring up a running virtual environment.

For the very first step, that is all that's needed. Although your virtual Ubuntu box right now, you can already bring it up by typing:

```
> vagrant up
```

This should result in an output similar to that shown in Listing 9-2.

Listing 9-2. *An Example Output After Starting Vagrant*

```
[default] Importing base box 'lucid32'...
[default] The guest additions on this VM do not match the
install version of VirtualBox! This may cause things such as
forwarded ports, shared folders, and more tonot work properly.
If any of those things fail on this machine, please update the
guest additions and repackage the box.

Guest Additions Version: 4.1.0
VirtualBox Version: 4.1.10
```

```
[default] Matching MAC address for NAT networking...
[default] Clearing any previously set forwarded ports...
[default] Forwarding ports...
[default] -- 22 => 2222 (adapter 1)
[default] Creating shared folders metadata...
[default] Clearing any previously set network interfaces...
[default] Booting VM...
[default] Waiting for VM to boot. This can take a few minutes.
[default] VM booted and ready for use!
[default] Mounting shared folders...
[default] -- v-root: /vagrant
```

You can see that Vagrant first imports and checks the base box (ignore the warning for the moment), sets up port forwarding and shared folders, and then boots the virtual machine. The folder with the Vagrant file gets mounted as a shared folder in the virtual machine under /vagrant.

Congratulations, you've successfully created your first Vagrant virtual environment! Now you likely want to log in to it and do some interesting stuff. As we saw in the log output in Listing 9-2, Vagrant created a port forwarding from the guest (the virtual machine, VM in short) port 22 to the host (your machine) port 2222, so that is an option to log in with Vagrant's default account (every Vagrant box has a user vagrant with the password vagrant). The more standard way to log in to any Vagrant box is to type:

```
> vagrant ssh
```

in the command line and you will be logged in.

With the default setup, your box is not visible to the outside, except the default port forwarding. However, to use it as a test system, you'll need more components to be accessible to you. One way to achieve this is to define your own port forwarding. Let's assume we want to set up a web server on the box and make it available via the host port 8001. That would look like this in the Vagrant file:

```
Vagrant::Config.run do |config|
config.vm.box = "lucid32"
config.vm.forward_port 80, 8001
end
```

To make this change in your configuration visible, reload your Vagrant environment:

```
> vagrant reload
```

This will shut down and reboot the box with the new configuration. Now, log in to your box, install Apache, and you'll be able to see the web server default page at http://localhost:8001.

```
> vagrant shh
lucid32> sudo apt-get update
lucid32> sudo apt-get install apache2
lucid32> nano /var/www/index.html
```

Finally, if you don't need your environment anymore, you can halt, suspend, or destroy it:

```
> vagrant halt|suspend|destroy
```

Halting and suspending preserves the state of your VM (i.e., the underlying VirtualBox VM will not be removed). If you destroy a box, all changes you made will be lost.

Host-Only Networking, Multi-VM Environments

You might already have thought that setting up port forwarding for every component on your test system is not really efficient, and you're right. Besides that, one of our initial goals was to create production-like environments in order to eliminate configuration errors early. Speaking of production-like, it is not realistic to believe that all your services will be running on one host only, so it would also be nice to handle several VMs with one Vagrant file. Fortunately, Vagrant addresses all these issues in the form of host-only networking and multi-VM environments.

As the name indicates, multi-VM environments let you handle several boxes with one Vagrant file. If you define more than one box in Vagrant, you need to add the name of the box to the Vagrant commands in order to let it know which box to boot, destroy, ssh in, and so forth. Most of the commands work without a name and will then be applied to all boxes defined in the current Vagrant file.

The other feature, host-only networking, enables you to assign static IP addresses to your VMs that are only accessible from the host machine. As long as you do not configure separate netmasks for the boxes, they can also see each other.

Listing 9-3 shows an example for both of these features.

Listing 9-3. *Example for Host-Only Networking, Multi-VM Environments*

```
Vagrant::Config.run do |config|
    config.vm.box = "lucid32"
    config.vm.box_url = "http://files.vagrantup.com/lucid32.box"
    config.vm.define :web do |web|
        web.vm.network :hostonly, "33.33.33.11"
    end
    config.vm.define :db do |db|
        db.vm.network :hostonly, "33.33.33.12"
    end
end
```

Running the Up command creates two VMs. You can log in to them with:

```
> vagrant ssh web|db
```

Both virtual machines are reachable from your computer under the specified IP addresses.

Provisioning with Puppet

As we have now covered the basics, we can finally get to the point this is all about: handling the set up of your infrastructure as code. Up until now, we only created some lightweight virtual machines. That's handy, but ultimately, we want to create machines complete with software and configuration.

As Vagrant also offers a mechanism to configure provisioning, we'll stick to it to introduce the next tool, Puppet. As mentioned before, Puppet is a configuration management tool, based on Ruby. It allows you to create so-called manifests, which include a description of the system in question.

Vagrant also allows you to use other provisioning tools, like Chef,[7] or do provisioning with shell scripts, but we will concentrate on Puppet here.

Let's get back to the small Apache web server example we used above to check that our VM was up and running and rebuild it with the help of Puppet. First, we need to tell Vagrant that it should use Puppet for provisioning and where it can find the Puppet manifest, as shown in Listing 9-4:

Listing 9-4. *Configure Puppet in Vagrant*

```
Vagrant::Config.run do |config|
  config.vm.box = "lucid32"
  config.vm.box_url = "http://files.vagrantup.com/lucid32.box"
  config.vm.network :hostonly, "33.33.33.10"
  config.vm.provision :puppet do |puppet|
  puppet.manifests_path = "manifests"
  puppet.manifest_file  = "webserver.pp"
end
```

We tell Vagrant to look for the Puppet manifests in the manifests folder and to use the file webserver.pp there. Before we take a closer look at the content of this manifest, let's quickly look at how Puppet works. Puppet uses a domain-specific language to describe a system in the form of resources. A resource can be nearly anything, from plain files, to software packages, services, or even command executions. These resources can then be grouped together in classes, modules, and node definitions. Visit the excellent online documentation for Puppet to learn more.

This is what a Puppet resource looks like:

```
<resource type> { "resource-name":
 attribute_name => attribute_value,
 ...
}
```

It consists of a certain resource type (e.g., file, group), a name, and a series of attributes in the form of key-value pairs. With these basics in mind, let's take a look at our web server manifest, as shown in Listing 9-5:

Listing 9-5. *Puppet Manifest Configuring the Web Server*

```
# to fix missing puppet group in lucid32 box
group { "puppet":
 ensure => present,
}

# to update outdated package list
exec { "refresh-packages":
```

---

[7] http://www.opscode.com/chef.

```
command => "/usr/bin/apt-get update",
before => Package["apache2"],
}

package { "apache2":
 ensure => installed,
}

service { "apache2":
 ensure => running,
 require => Package["apache2"],
}

file { "/var/www/index.html":
 ensure => file,
 content => "<html><body><h1>Vagrant and Puppet rocks!</h1></body></html>",
 require => Service["apache2"],
}
```

The first resource states that a group with the name puppet should be present on the system in question. If this is not the case, Puppet will go on and create that group. The ensure parameter can be found on many Puppet resources to specify the desired state for the resource. The next resource is a command execution to refresh the Ubuntu package repository list. The next two resources tell Puppet that the operating system's underlying package manager should install the 'apache2' package if it is not installed yet and that the related service should be running. Finally, the last resource alters the content of the default Apache index page.

You might notice that some resources have parameters like before and require the so-called metaparameters. They indicate dependencies between resources for Puppet, as it has by itself no guaranteed execution order for its resources. The dependency between the package and the service is typical, because obviously the package needs to be installed before Puppet can check if the related service is up and running.

If you start this virtual machine now, you'll see some more output in contrast to running Vagrant without provisioning, and after everything is finished, you can go to http://33.33.33.10 and see the modified index page.

Using Vagrant for Continuous Integration

While reading through the above, you might already have thought about integrating these tools into your continuous integration setup to create test environments on the fly. If you use the popular Jenkins CI server, there's already a plug-in, written by Tyler Croy. It adds new build steps to Jenkins to run and provision Vagrant boxes during build jobs. Just use Jenkins plug-in management page to install the plug-in, then create a new job and configure it as shown in Figure 9-2.

Build Environment
_____

☑ Boot Vagrant box

Path to Vagrantfile   ./vagrant-jenkins/

         Alternate path, relative to workspace root, to Vagrantfile (*only needed if the Vagrantfile is not in the root directory*)

Build
_____

▦ **Provision the Vagrant machine**

                                               [Delete]

▦ **Execute shell**   ❓

Command   `curl 127.0.0.1:8181/test`

  See the list of available environment variables

                                             [Delete]

[Add build step ▼]

| Execute Windows batch command |
| Execute shell |
| Execute shell script in Vagrant |
| Execute shell script in Vagrant as admin |
| Invoke Ant |
| Invoke top-level Maven targets |
| Provision the Vagrant machine |

[Save] [Apply]

Figure 9-2. *Configuration of Vagrant as Jenkins Build Job*

You can see we've ticked the box to tell Jenkins to run Vagrant during the job and told it where to find the Vagrant file. Then, in the build itself, the provisioning step of Vagrant is executed (it isn't while booting the box here) and finally, we use cURL, a command line tool for transferring data (see http://curl.haxx.se), to check if the web server is up and running and serves our demo index page.

If you run this job and go to the console output in Jenkins, you can see all of the above steps executed, as shown in Figure 9-3.

Jenkins > Vagrant-Plugin Test > #8

◆ Previous Build

```
Seen branch in repository origin/HEAD
Seen branch in repository origin/master
Commencing build of Revision c797d696f7851f0f7b15e723db3d88f5c6483bf2a (origin/HEAD, origin/master)
Checking out Revision c797d696f7851f0f7b15e723db3d88f5c6483bf2a (origin/HEAD, origin/master)
Warning : There are multiple branch changesets here
Running Vagrant with version: 1.0.2.dev
Vagrantfile loaded, bringing Vagrant box up for the build
Importing base box 'lucid32'.
The guest additions on this VM do not match the install version of
VirtualBox! This may cause things such as forwarded ports, shared
folders, and more to not work properly. If any of those things fail on
this machine, please update the guest additions and repackage the
box.

Guest Additions Version: 4.1.0
VirtualBox Version: 4.1.10
Matching MAC address for NAT networking...
Clearing any previously set forwarded ports...
Forwarding ports...
-- 22 => 2222 (adapter 1)
-- 8080 => 8181 (adapter 1)
Creating shared folders metadata...
Clearing any previously set network interfaces...
Booting VM...
Waiting for VM to boot. This can take a few minutes.
VM booted and ready for use!
Setting host name...
Mounting shared folders...
-- v-root: /vagrant
-- manifests: /tmp/vagrant-puppet/manifests
Vagrant box is online, continuing with the build
Provisioning the Vagrant VM.. (this may take a while)
Running provisioner: Vagrant::Provisioners::Puppet...
Running Puppet with /tmp/vagrant-puppet/manifests/site.pp...
stdin: is not a tty
[0;36mnotice: /Group|puppet|/ensure: created[0m

[0;36mnotice: /Stage|main|/Exec|update-package-lists|/returns: executed successfully[0m
[0;36mnotice: /Stage|main|/Java/Package|openjdk-6-jdk|/ensure: ensure changed 'purged' to 'present'[0m
[0;36mnotice: /Stage|main|/Tomcat/Package|tomcat6|/ensure: ensure changed 'purged' to 'present'[0m
[0;36mnotice: /Stage|main|/Tomcat/File|/var/lib/tomcat6/webapps/test.war|/ensure: defined content as
'{md5}45ae7be1472ff25b632605e453b0bd91'[0m

[0;36mnotice: /Stage|main|/Tomcat/Service|tomcat6|: Triggered 'refresh' from 1 events[0m
[0;36mnotice: Finished catalog run in 137.87 seconds[0m

[workspace] $ /bin/sh -xe /home/bs/software/jenkins/server/temp/hudson8141041880438560445.sh
+ curl 127.0.0.1:8181/test
% Total    % Received % Xferd  Average Speed   Time    Time     Time  Current
                                 Dload  Upload   Total   Spent    Left  Speed
  0     0    0     0    0     0      0      0 --:--:-- --:--:-- --:--:--     0
100   156    0   156    0     0    996      0 --:--:-- --:--:-- --:--:--   993
100   156    0   156    0     0    995      0 --:--:-- --:--:-- --:--:--   993
<html><head><title>Jenkins-Vagrant-Demo</title></head><body><h1>The Jenkins-Vagrant-Plugin is awesome!
</h1><p>Mon Apr 23 15:13:29 PDT 2012</p></body></html>Build finished, destroying the Vagrant box
Forcing shutdown of VM...
Destroying VM and associated drives...
Finished: SUCCESS
```

Figure 9-3. *Jenkins Build Job Output*

In a real-world scenario, you would likely mix several projects in this build: the one holding your infrastructure specification and the Vagrant file, the application you want to test, maybe another project that includes some sort of deployment automation (e.g., with Maven and the cargo-plug-in), and finally some sort of acceptance or integration test project that would get executed against the virtual environment.

With this type of setup, differences in configuration for all the environments can be found early and get eliminated before they cause problems later on.

At the time of writing, the Vagrant plug-in for Jenkins is still in an early stage of development. In tests, host-only networks didn't work reliably at this early moment in its development, but nonetheless the plug-in can already be very helpful to give faster feedback to your developers and system administrators. Also, as it is open source, just go over to GitHub[8] and start contributing if you find any bugs.

Complementary Tools

What else is there to say about Vagrant? Until now, we only used the Ubuntu base box that is available from the Vagrant web site, but it is likely you want to use other operating systems to set up your own environments. There is documentation on how to build your own boxes with VirtualBox and package them for later reuse on the Vagrant home page. Another option is to check out http://vagrantbox.es, a web site that lists boxes (i.e., templates for different operating systems) that have been built by members of the Vagrant community and posted for download.

A third option is to use the open source tool Veewee,[9] which makes building new base boxes for Vagrant even easier. Since version 1.0, Vagrant also offers support for writing plug-ins, and it remains to be seen what will evolve there. Check out the Vagrant page for more information (see http://vagrantup.com/). There are also links to an Internet relay chat channel and a Google group, where you'll find like-minded people willing to help.

You can edit Puppet manifests and modules with a simple text editor, but to have autocompletion and other nice features you may prefer to use Geppetto,[10] which is build on Eclipse. You can check that Puppet manifests conform to the style guide with puppet-lint.[11] Another helpful tool is guard-puppet,[12] which helps to reapply Puppet configs automatically.

Tools like Cucumber-Puppet[13] and puppet-rspec[14] help to test your manifests. They let you write Cucumber and RSpec tests for your manifests in order to make sure all of them comply to your manifest policies. With puppet-rspec, tests follow the following structure:

```
require 'spec_helper'
describe '<name of the thing being tested>' do
  # Your tests go in here
end
```

---

[8] https://github.com/.
[9] https://github.com/jedi4ever/veewee.
[10] https://github.com/cloudsmith/geppetto.
[11] https://github.com/rodjek/puppet-lint.
[12] http://rubygems.org/gems/guard-puppet.
[13] http://projects.puppetlabs.com/projects/cucumber-puppet.
[14] https://github.com/rodjek/rspec-puppet.

All these neat tools help to apply the practice of test-driven development (TDD)[15] to Puppet manifests and to add Puppet manifests to your continuous integration and continuous delivery system.

Provisioning with Puppet

We saw the benefits of using Puppet to manage virtual environments together with Vagrant. This is already quite useful for development teams and also can be used to set up and tear down QA environments as needed. But there is a lot more to Puppet, and its actual role is to manage every type of environment, be it development or production. Let's take a look at how to set up a Puppet server that stores the configuration for all of its managed nodes in a central place and distributes them as needed.

Setting Up a Puppet Master

To get started, we first need to install Puppet on the local system, which will be our Puppet master. This is the host that runs Puppet in the server mode and listens for Puppet agents to pull their configuration from there. In Ubuntu, the installation is quite simple:

```
> sudo apt-get install puppet
```

This installs Puppet on your local machine and puts configuration files into /etc/puppet. As I aim to make the examples simple, we enable autosigning of new Puppet clients, to avoid signing and exchanging certificates between the Puppet master and the clients. In a production environment you should not do this. To enable autosigning, put a file autosign.conf into /etc/puppet, containing the following content:

```
*.example.com
```

This will automatically sign all certificate requests from clients with a matching hostname (e.g., web01.example.com) and remove the extra step of doing a certificate exchange before master and client can communicate with each other. Now, restart the Puppet master to make our change visible:

```
> sudo /etc/init.d/puppetmaster restart
```

Setting Up a Puppet Client

Now we're ready to set up a host that acts as a Puppet client. Again, we use Vagrant to set up a host. Just create a new Vagrant file, with the content shown in Listing 9-6:

Listing 9-6. *Configure a Puppet Client*

```
Vagrant::Config.run do |config|
  config.vm.box = "lucid32"
  config.vm.box_url = "http://files.vagrantup.com/lucid32.box"
```

---

[15] http://www.jedi.be/blog/2011/12/13/testdriven-infrastructure-with-vagrant-puppet-guard/.

```
config.vm.network :hostonly, "33.33.33.33"
config.vm.host_name = "node01.example.com"
end
```

Boot this box and ssh into it. To finally enable it to connect to your Puppet master, we have to add an entry with the Puppet master's IP address and hostname to the box /etc/hosts. Additionally, we need to add a group 'puppet' to the system, which is missing in the lucid32 box. Now your virtual host can run the Puppet agent. Normally the agent would daemonize and run periodically in the background to ask the master for up-to-date configuration. To illustrate what happens behind the scene, we're going to run things by hand here.

```
> puppet agent --test --server <puppetmaster hostname>
```

This should result in output similar to Listing 9-7:

Listing 9-7. *Output of Testing the Puppet Agent*

```
info: Creating a new SSL key for node01.example.com
warning: peer certificate won't be verified in this SSL session
info: Caching certificate for ca
warning: peer certificate won't be verified in this SSL session
info: Creating a new SSL certificate request for
node01.example.com
info: Certificate Request fingerprint (md5):
1F:7D:07:3E:FC:0E:8F:67:18:A6:DC:8D:DE:E7:4A:2E
warning: peer certificate won't be verified in this SSL session
info: Caching certificate for node01.example.com
info: Caching certificate_revocation_list for ca
err: Could not retrieve catalog from remote server: Error 400 on
SERVER: Could not find default node or by name with
'node01.example.com, node01.example, node01' on node
node01.example.com
warning: Not using cache on failed catalog
err: Could not retrieve catalog; skipping run
```

You see the agent and master exchange certificates and that the master tries to find a catalog for the requesting node. As we haven't yet configured anything, the agent doesn't receive any information and aborts the run. If the agent would be daemonized and run in the background, it would poll the master in a configured interval to ask if a new or changed catalog is available. If that is the case, the catalog will get executed on the client.

Now, let's write a simple node definition. On your local machine, go to /etc/puppet/manifests and create a folder for nodes. Then edit the file /etc/puppet/manifests/site.pp and add this line:

```
import 'nodes/*'
```

This tells Puppet to import all files in the nodes folder, and this is where we will put our node definition. Create a file nodes/node01.pp with the content given in Listing 9-8:

Listing 9-8. *Creating a Node, with Puppet*

```
node 'node01.example.com' {
  file { "/tmp/test.txt":
  ensure => file,
  content => "It works!",
  }
}
```

If you rerun Puppet on the agent host, you will see that the Puppet master delivers a catalog to the client that is executed there. In this simple case, we will see the file test.txt after the execution.

After going through the features and benefits of Vagrant and Puppet, we are now ready to discover how a real-world project, the Jenkins CI build server, runs those tools in its DevOps approach.

Use Case: Open Source Infrastructure with Puppet

Have you ever downloaded a .jar file from some ASF (Apache Software Foundation) project, downloaded a Debian .iso from kernel.org, or maybe just read an article on Wikipedia? Have you ever stopped to think about how those bits get from one place to you? Who runs those machines, sets up those networks, receives those pages when all of that breaks?

Functional infrastructure is an oft overlooked but necessary component of the thriving open source ecosystem. In the examples above, there are probably a few people whose part- or full-time job it is to care for and tend to those systems.

Those are all big, important projects though, so what about the rest of us?

The Need, from the Jenkins Viewpoint

For a project such as Jenkins (http://jenkins-ci.org), the infrastructure needs had grown large enough so it no longer fit on a "forge" or could comfortably be hosted on some community member's Linode instance. Jenkins has multiple machines in multiple locations, such as the OSUOSL (http://osuosl.org) and even in Amazon's EC2.

Initially Jenkins had done things the old-fashioned way, that is to say the wrong way: manually handcrafting machine after machine and tweaking configurations until things appeared to work on machines in production. This continued until a (very) costly misconfiguration caused a single machine to inadvertently serve many terabytes of data more than it was supposed to, an expensive mistake Jenkins only noticed and corrected after someone received an overage bill.

After this "event," Jenkins started to incorporate Puppet into their management toolkit to meet a few crucial goals. The infrastructure should be:

- Testable (outside of production of course)

- Auditable

- Transparent

Unfortunately, migrating existing, handcrafted, infrastructure over to be managed by Puppet has been a long and tedious process. Imagine rebuilding a jet engine, midflight, while trying to maintain a steady altitude; that's hard.

The How at Jenkins

From the beginning, the Jenkins Puppet work has been married to Vagrant. Vagrant integrates neatly with Puppet and allows a user to effortlessly bring up a Linux-based virtual machine and provision it with Puppet. Let's go into more details about the different aspects.

Running Puppet

Puppet can be run in one of two ways: in a client-server architecture and with "stand-alone mode," the former being the far more common use case. The client-server model has its benefits, such as being able to push changes immediately, or gather so-called facts from all your nodes, but for Jenkins a stand-alone mode is used.

Jenkins wanted to introduce a way to remove additional service dependencies; being in multiple locations means you have one of two options with the client-server model: introduce a single point of failure in one location, or deploy a Puppet master to each location.

There is also a question of simplicity; since Vagrant integrates with Puppet by utilizing this stand-alone mode, Jenkins effectively tests their manifests locally in a manner much more consistent with the production environment.

The Tradeoffs

As you might expect, giving up the client-server model means Jenkins had to duplicate some functionality themselves. For example, since Jenkins cannot push updates to machines, Jenkins has a module for autoupdating each machine from Git. This module, shown in Listing 9-9, manages the periodical pulling of updates from the Git repository and running each machine's root[16] manifest:

Listing 9-9. *Managing Git Pull Requests and Running Root Manifest*

```
class autoupdate {
    include autoupdate::setup
    Class["autoupdate::setup"] -> Class["autoupdate"]

    cron {
        "pull puppet updates" :
            command     => "(cd /root/infra-puppet && sh run.sh)",
            user        => root,
```

---

[16] According to the current solution how Jenkins hosts its own production system at http://jenkins-ci.org, the root user is used. Often it is considered to be a good practice to not use the root user and create and use a dedicated user instead.

```
              minute      => 15,
              ensure      => present;

        # Might as well clean these up at some point
        "clean up old puppet logs" :
              command     => "rm -f /root/infra-puppet/puppet.*.log",
              user        => root,
              hour        => 4,
              minute      => 30,
              weekday     => '*',
              ensure      => present;
    } }

class autoupdate::setup {
    exec {
        "setup_git_repo" :
            cwd     => "/root",
            creates => "/root/infra-puppet",
            command => "git clone git://github.com/jenkinsci/infra-puppet.git",
            require => Package["git-core"],
            # In the case of a new machine, we probably already have this
            unless  => "test -d /root/infra-puppet/.git",
            path    => ["/usr/bin", "/usr/local/bin"],
    }
}
```

Also because Jenkins is not using the client-server module, this means Jenkins can't take advantage of some of the recent developments in Puppet module dependency management (example usage: http://puppetlabs.com/blog/using-puppet-modules-to-install-and-manage-wordpress). The approach taken has been to use Git submodules to manage the dependency on other modules to be reused, such as:

- puppetlabs-stdlib: common dependency for many of Puppet labs' modules

- puppetlabs-firewall: for managing iptables rules

- puppetlabs-ntp: for automatically setting up ntp, crons, and so forth

- puppet-sshd: for managing sshd_configs and keeping the daemons running

- puppet-concat: for managing or concatenating configurations for services that do not support conf.d/ style directories

- puppet-postgres: setting up PostgreSQL permissions, databases, and so forth

With puppet-module-tool,[17] Puppet can create, install, and search for modules on the Puppet Forge (see `http://forge.puppetlabs.com`), the place to find and share Puppet modules. The puppet-module-tool has been moved into core as of Puppet version 2.7.12.

Most Puppet modules are published to Puppet Forge, but their source typically lives on Github, making them easy to add as submodules, for example:

```
> cd project-root
> git submodule add git://github.com/puppetlabs/puppetlabs-firewall.git
modules/firewall
> git commit -m "Add the firewall module to manage iptables"
```

After it's been added to the tree, using it on a particular machine is easy enough (note: the firewall module adds some resources, some modules may require an "include" to use properly), as shown in Listing 9-10:

Listing 9-10. *Extending Our Configuration by Adding Firewall Settings*
```
firewall {
    '000 accept all icmp requests' :
        proto  => 'icmp',
        action => 'accept';

    '001 accept inbound ssh requests' :
        proto  => 'tcp',
        port   => 22,
        action => 'accept';

    # etc, etc
}
```

The submodule approach can be a double-edged sword and will cut you if you're not careful. On the one hand, you've got some level of built-in version freezing in adding the submodule. But if the submodule is updated too frequently or is under constant iteration, then you will litter the superproject with commits just to update the submodule reference.

Regardless of whether the client-server or stand-alone approach is used, reusing existing modules from the Puppet Forge is a good decision and can help bootstrap a project quickly, allowing you to focus on your specific needs instead of reinventing the wheel.

Source of Truth

One other major difference in this stand-alone setup compared to the client-server model is the "source of truth" for the machines managed by Puppet. In the traditional client-server architecture, the Puppet master is the boss, and what the boss says, goes. In the Jenkins setup, GitHub is our sole source of truth. This means that whatever the state of the "master" branch in our repository, that is the state of the machines (give or take 15 minutes).

The second major benefit of this approach is that Jenkins can easily accept contributions to the infrastructure by way of GitHub pull requests. You could submit a pull request (theoretically)

---

[17] `https://github.com/puppetlabs/puppet-module-tool`.

to add an entire new service on the Jenkins infrastructure, and it could be reviewed and merged without the "core" team ever giving you access to the hardware itself.

Testing with Vagrant

A lot of the flexibility Jenkins has derived from our Puppet setup hasn't come solely from Puppet, but the combination of Puppet and Vagrant. It's hard to imagine a more convenient way to set up a full BIND9 nameserver[18] in less than 40 minutes.

Jenkins needed a nameserver, and it needs a nameserver quickly. Fortunately, it already had an existing Puppet infrastructure set up, so it wasn't too much work to add the nameserver.

First things first; Jenkins created a branch to do the work in and then set up some folders (some paths changed to protect the innocent):

```
> git checkout -b build-a-nameserver-quick
> mkdir -p modules/bind/manifests modules/bind/files
> vim modules/bind/manifests/init.pp
```

After about 10 minutes of looking up package names, they had a basic set of resources defined to make up a simple BIND9-based nameserver, as shown in Listing 9-11:

Listing 9-11. *Adding BIND9 to Our Configuration*

```
# Skip the class declaration for now
package {
    'bind' :
        ensure => present, # Ensure the package is installed on Ubuntu
        name   => 'bind9';
}
service {
    "bind" :
        ensure  => running, # Ensure we have it up and running on boot
        require => Package['bind'],
        name    => 'bind9';
}
# Open up our firewall (provided by puppetlabs-firewall) to allow
# both TCP and UDP-based DNS traffic
firewall {
    "900 accept tcp DNS queries" :
        proto  => "tcp",
        port   => 53,
        action => "accept";
```

---

[18] BIND stands for Berkeley Internet Name Domain and is an implementation of the domain name system (DNS) protocol. More about BIND and its version 9 can be found at http://www.bind9.net.

```
"901 accept udp DNS queries" :
    proto  => "udp",
    port   => 53,
    action => "accept";
}
```

If you've ever set up BIND before, you know that getting things installed and running isn't the hard part. It's the confusing, fickle configuration files that are really difficult to get right. Using Vagrant, we would enter a tight bind-frustration-and-iteration loop:

```
> vagrant up # also provisions when the VM is online
> vagrant ssh # Log into our VM
# Check to make sure that everything looks right, oh wait, no it doesn't,
# why are you doing that BIND? Why! Argh! You're so stupid! Don't act like
# that or I'll shut you down, that's it!
> vagrant destroy # I'll show BIND who's boss!
> vim init.pp # Okay, where'd we go wrong.
```

In your case, you might not use the vagrant destroy command as much as Jenkins does, but it's hard to go too long without wiping the slate clean (which the 'destroy' command does) and starting all over again with just your pure Puppet manifests.

Around minute 35 of the "build a nameserver quick" project, Jenkins had things up and running and was running dig(1) from a local machine against the nameserver running inside the Vagrant VM, making final checks that everything was fully functional before sending code to GitHub:

```
> git commit modules/bind -m "Long and descriptive commit message should go here"
> git push origin
```

Within 15 minutes, the appropriate machine comes online and is a fully tested, code-reviewed, reproducible, and functional nameserver.

Full Circle

Unfortunately, the goal of the Jenkins project is not to build a textbook infrastructure, but rather to build one that works and stays working, so Jenkins can focus on building a stellar CI server (which Puppet Labs uses, we might add here: http://jenkins.puppetlabs.com). We can go back every day and figure out how and why things are the way they are, and it's all right there in the Git repository.

Thanks to Puppet, with a dash of Vagrant, a lot of things "just work" without much hand-holding, and that's how Jenkins is able to have a big infrastructure without a big-time investment.

Where to Look Next?

Puppet can be used together with Augeas[19] to enable you to alter existing files without the need to use templates.

---

[19] http://augeas.net.

If you start using Puppet with a number of hosts, you might want to look closer at the Puppet Dashboard, a web application that lets you monitor the state of all your Puppet-managed nodes.

You may want to take a look at PuppetDB,[20] which is a Puppet data warehouse to manage, storage, and retrieve all platform-generated data.

There are also many existing Puppet modules created by the community that you can find in the Puppet Forge, a repository of reusable Puppet modules.

All of the mentioned tools offer extensive documentation on their web pages and have either mailing lists, Google groups, Internet relay chat channels, or even all of them. Take a look at their web sites for more information.

If you are looking for further literature on Puppet, there are two recent books available: *Pro Puppet* by James Turnbull and Jeffrey McCune (Apress, 2011) and the *Puppet 2.7 Cookbook* by John Arundel (Packt Publishing, 2011). The former gives a good overall introduction to Puppet, also covering advanced topics and a lot of best practices. The latter contains a lot of small and easy-to-reuse recipes to solve your everyday Puppet problems.

Alternatives

With Vagrant and Puppet, we've examined two tools that can help to aid your development, testing, and operations. The choice of these, however, was based solely on my personal preferences, and there are many other configuration management frameworks out there, with the other two big open source tools being CFEngine[21] and Chef.

CFEngine is the oldest of these open source tools, with initial efforts dating back as early as 1993. The initial releases of Puppet and Chef are from 2005 and 2009, respectively. Due to its age, CFEngine is probably most widespread, however, in recent years, both Chef and Puppet gained a strong community and are used by a lot of startups and younger companies. There are also a lot of tools evolving from these two, addressing topics like integrated drive electronics or test-driven development, which may make these two more worthy of consideration. Just take some time to look into them and see which one you like better.

There are also commercial and a lot of lesser known frameworks and tools available. Check out Wikipedia or your usual development forum for more hints.

Conclusion

We've only scratched the surface of the possibilities provided by the tools addressed in this chapter. There is a lot more to be discovered, and I hope this has stirred your curiosity about using these or similar tools.

With configuration management and the infrastructure as code paradigm in general, the collaboration of development and operations is no longer merely a possibility, but almost a necessary. After all, every developer needs to know his or her share of system administration, and every system administrator has to learn about the components the architects and developers choose to run their application. The tools described here can greatly improve the sharing of knowledge between the two groups and help to make the DevOps movement even more successful.

Let's now proceed to the last chapter of this book that discusses acceptance tests.

---

[20] docs.puppetlabs.com/puppetdb.
[21] http://cfengine.com.

Specification by Example

48% of devops are automate their test. 12% are test their automation. 3% are do both.

—DevOps Borat[1]

One of the fundamental principles of DevOps is that any build that successfully passes the gauntlet of automated checks can potentially be delivered into production. Checks can specifically verify whether any new or updated code broke any existing feature. In other words, they guard against regression failures. It is for this reason that automated testing plays such a vital role in the DevOps process.

However, there is much more to automated testing than just running a set of unit tests on a build server. It is not enough to simply have a suite of automated tests: if you intend to automatically deliver a product into production, every team member must also be convinced of the quality of these tests, in the sense of whether the tests truly capture what the customers desired in the product and whether the tests have any informative expressiveness to help developers develop the solution.

In this chapter, we'll discuss acceptance tests with the use of the free tool Thucydides.[2] We'll see that acceptance tests are a good choice to foster collaboration between development and operations by providing an executable specification of the developed software. The tool Thucydides is a great choice to implement these tests.

Getting Started with Acceptance Tests

When a tester delegates parts of her manual testing activity to a suite of automated tests, she may fear some loss of control when the whole team engages in creating executable acceptance

---

[1] http://twitter.com/devops_borat/status/202501609828257792.
[2] For more information about Thucydides, see http://thucydides.net/.

tests. It's often a difficult process to understand acceptance tests as a good way to do testing. Developers (including testers) collaborate as a team to capture the customer desires in the form of executable tests, and once they pass, the team turns those into regression checks.

One major benefit of acceptance tests is transparency. The product owner should be able to know precisely which features are being delivered in a particular release, including what works (and what doesn't). The business analyst should be able to see exactly how the stories have been implemented. And the operations team will want to know exactly which features are being delivered into production, as they will be expected to support them. A medium is needed to foster communication between all stakeholders, and that medium can be the acceptance tests, which we'll discuss next.

Acceptance Tests as a Communication Vehicle

This focus on communication is typical of automated acceptance testing and of techniques such as acceptance test-driven development in particular. Indeed, automated acceptance testing is as much about publishing and communicating the results of the tests as it is about executing the tests.

ACCEPTANCE TEST-DRIVEN DEVELOPMENT

Acceptance test-driven development (ATDD) is an advanced form of test-driven development (TDD) in which automated acceptance criteria—defined in collaboration with users—drive and focus the development process. This helps ensure that everyone understands which features are under development. This chapter covers the essential basics of ATDD, by example.

In fact, the idea of specifying acceptance tests before starting the development work is not new. During the 1980s, the V model of software development proposed a tight coupling between the specifications, written at the start of the project, and the acceptance tests, carried out at the end. However, it is only in recent years that software tools and practices have emerged that make it feasible to automate these acceptance criteria from the word go.

There are many ways to communicate the outcomes of your acceptance tests, and the best solution will obviously vary from team to team and from project to project. In this chapter, we will look at one such solution. Thucydides is an open source library designed to make writing and reporting automated acceptance and regression tests easier. It provides features that help you organize and structure your acceptance criteria, associating them with the user stories or features that they test. And when the tests are executed, Thucydides generates detailed reports, including high-level views of the overall test outcomes as well as detailed step-by-step documentation describing how the application implements the features it is supposed to deliver.

Let's now start our roundtrip through acceptance tests with Thucydides by defining acceptance criteria.

Defining Your Acceptance Criteria

One of the key concepts behind ATDD and automated acceptance testing in general is the idea of specification by example.[3] Specification by example refers to the use of relatively concrete examples to illustrate how a system should work, as opposed to more formally written specifications expressed in very general terms.

Let's look at an example. Suppose we are working on a web site that posts classified ads online (see Figure 10-1). In many projects, requirements are expressed as simple user stories like the following:

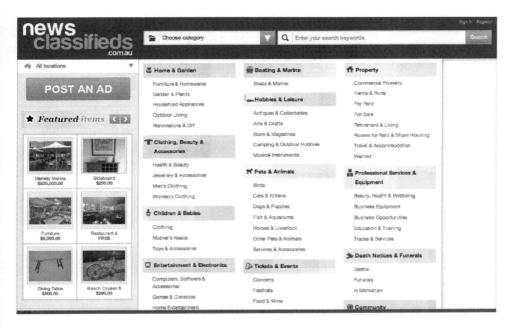

Figure 10-1. *An online classifieds web site*

- In order to find the best deal, as a buyer, I want to see all the available ads in a particular category.

- In order to find the items I am interested in faster, as a buyer, I want to be able to list all the ads with a particular keyword in the description or title.

- In order to find an item that I can afford, as a buyer, I want to be able to filter ads in a particular category by price range.

- In order to reduce postage costs, as a buyer, I want to be able to list only the ads in a particular region.

---

[3] See Gojko Adzik, *Specification by Example* (Manning, 2011).

To clarify these requirements, we would then agree on a list of acceptance criteria for each of them. In a first pass, we would list a set of key examples that illustrate and clarify each story. For example, as part of our list, we might come up with some of the following:

- In order to find the best deal, as a buyer, I want to see all the available ads in a particular category.

- In order to find the items I am interested in faster, as a buyer, I want to be able to list all the ads with a particular keyword in the description or title.

- List all the ads in the "Home and Garden" category.

- List all of the ads containing the word "puppy" in the "Pets and Animals" category.

- List all of the properties for rent between $400 and $500.

- List all of the properties for sale in New South Wales.

These are concrete examples that help to give a clearer picture of the requirements. These examples also lead to discussion about the details and scope of the requirements. For instance, we might find that searching by keyword will be more useful when restricted to the ads of a given category. As a result, the example we provide ("List all of the ads containing the word 'puppy' in the 'Pets and Animals' category") illustrates that idea.

Elaborating the Examples

Once we have defined our acceptance criteria, we refine these examples into a more structured form, which will make it easier to automate in the next phase. A common approach is to elaborate examples using a "given-when-then" structure. This puts the focus on the action and the expected outcome. For example, based on the examples above, we might come up with the following:

Given Sally wants to buy a puppy for her son
When she looks for ads in the "Pets and Animals" category containing the word "puppy"
Then she should obtain a list of ads related to puppies.

Or

Given that Joe wants to rent an apartment in his budget
When he looks for "To Rent" ads in the "Property" category between $400 and $500
Then he should obtain a list containing only "To Rent" ads in this price range.

Note that these requirements focus on the business value of each feature, without delving into the details of how these features will actually be implemented, or, for that matter, tested. The emphasis is on what business outcome is expected, rather than on how it will be obtained.

Automating the Acceptance Criteria

Once we have formalized our acceptance criteria, we can automate them. This involves implementing the acceptance criteria as an automated test, which can be run as part of the automated build process. Naturally, when we first run the test, it will fail, as the feature in question will not have been implemented yet.

When using Thucydides, we would typically use a behavior-driven development (BDD) tool such as easyb[4] or JBehave[5] for this purpose. As Dan North states, "Behavior-driven development (BDD) takes the position that you can turn an idea for a requirement into implemented, tested, production-ready code simply and effectively, as long as the requirement is specific enough that everyone knows what's going on" and "BDD uses a story as the basic unit of functionality, and therefore of delivery. The acceptance criteria are an intrinsic part of the story."[6] Although by no means indispensable, specialized BDD tools make it easier and more natural to express automated acceptance criteria using a language and structure that is readily understandable by nondevelopers.

Throughout the rest of this chapter, we will be using easyb to illustrate the principles of ATDD with Thucydides. A similar approach could also be used for other BDD tools such as JBehave.

In easyb, a simple automated scenario would look like this:

```
scenario "List all of the ads containing the word 'puppy' in the 'Pets and
animals' category", {
    given "Sally wants to buy a puppy for her son"
    when "she looks for ads in the 'Pets and Animals' category containing the
word 'puppy'"
    then "she should see a list of ads related to puppies."
}
```

To integrate this story into Thucydides, we would add some more details, including which feature this acceptance criteria relates to. We do this by adding a few extra lines to the scenario, as in Listing 10-1:

Listing 10-1. *Integrating the Story into Thucydides*

```
using "thucydides"
thucydides.tests.feature "Search ads"
scenario "List all of the ads containing the word 'puppy' in the 'Pets and
animals' category", {
    given "Sally wants to buy a puppy for her son"
    when "she looks for ads in the 'Pets and Animals' category containing the
word 'puppy'"
    then "she should see a list of ads related to puppies."
}
```

---

[4]www.easyb.org.
[5]www.jbehave.org.
[6]See http://dannorth.net/whats-in-a-story/ for more details about BDD.

In a similar manner, we would elaborate and automate the other acceptance criteria that we intend to implement. This typically happens at the start of an iteration or sprint and gives a clear picture of which features will be implemented in the current sprint and which acceptance criteria must be met for each of them.

In Thucydides, acceptance criteria are typically organized into arbitrary groupings such as features, behaviors, or whatever other division makes sense to the product owner. This makes it easier to obtain a higher-level view of where a project is at and what is ready to be delivered.

Once automated, the acceptance criteria pass from mere text documents to being executable specifications. We can run them during the automated build process and generate a report similar to the one in Figure 10-2, which gives a high-level overview of the state of the acceptance

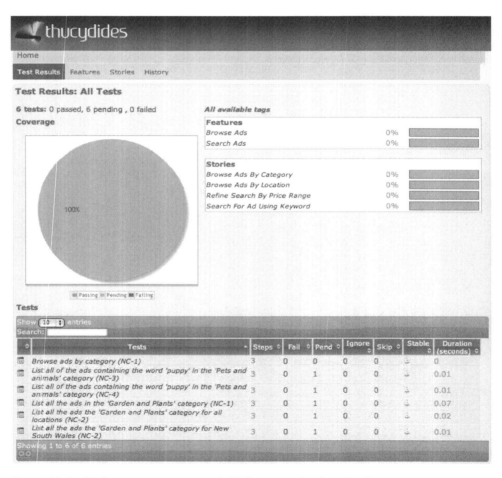

Figure 10-2. *All the acceptance tests are initially reported as "pending"*

criteria. These reports also make it easy to drill down into a particular feature or functional area, in order to get a more detailed view about the state of readiness of that feature. In our example, some tests are still pending. That's an important point and it depends on when tests get written. Scenarios are first written as "pending." These are just high-level outlines, describing a set of acceptance criteria for a particular story in a given-when-then structure. When the tests are executed, pending scenarios are skipped. However, they appear in the reports, so you know which features still need to be implemented.

It often works best to write tests as coding begins or just before. Teams could get in trouble writing a lot of detailed executable tests before any code is written and also if they wait too late to write them. They should experiment to find the right timing.

Implementing the Tests

The next step is to implement these stories so they actually perform the tests they are supposed to do. Since we are testing a web application, it makes sense to implement at least some of the acceptance criteria using automated web testing. Indeed, as web application design becomes more sophisticated and interactive, it is increasingly important to implement these tests.

We could now implement the story described above directly using a web testing library such as Selenium 2.[7] However this would result in a large number of low-level details appearing in the automated acceptance criteria, which tends to make the automated acceptance criteria brittle and hard to maintain. It is far better to keep these details well away from our functional specifications.

After we've written high-level tests, we can now proceed to the step where we slice these high-level tests into fine-grained steps.

Slice High-Level Tests into Steps

When we implement this acceptance criteria, we start by breaking them down into logical steps. These steps are still expressed in high-level business terms, without too much implementation detail. They aim to express how a user is expected to achieve the corresponding business goal, without delving too far into the implementation details. This step is often done at the start of an iteration or just before work starts on a feature, as a collaborative exercise between a developer, a tester, and a product owner or business analyst.

For example, elaborating the acceptance criteria we have been considering so far, the team might come up with the following more detailed scenario in Thucydides, where I've added references to step classes and thus also an `import` statement for these classes, as shown in Listing 10-2:

Listing 10-2. *A more detailed example containing a scenario*

```
import com.acme.onlineclassifieds.webtests.steps.BuyerSteps
using "thucydides"
thucydides.tests.feature "Search ads"
thucydides.uses_default_base_url "http://my.staging.server"
thucydides.uses_steps_named("sally").from BuyerSteps
```

---

[7]See http://seleniumhq.org/

```
scenario "List all of the ads containing the word 'puppy' in the 'Pets and
animals' category", {
    given "Sally wants to buy a puppy for her son"
    when "she looks for ads in the 'Pets and Animals' category containing the
word 'puppy'", {
        sally.opens_home_page()
        sally.chooses_category "Pets & Animals"
        sally.looks_for_ads_containing_keywords "puppy"
    }
    then "she should see a list of ads related to puppies.", {
        sally.should_only_see_results_with_titles_containing "puppy"
    }
}
```

This approach has two main advantages. First, the implementation of the acceptance tests remains highly readable for nondevelopers. When acceptance criteria are written in this way, their intent is immediately clear. Second, these steps become building blocks that can be reused in other tests, which makes the tests faster to write and easier to maintain.

Table-Driven Tests

In other situations, several slightly different examples might be needed to illustrate a particular feature. For example, consider a scenario where regular customers can obtain a special gold card that gives them access to different discount rates, based on the number of points accumulated on their cards. To cater to this sort of case, most BDD tools also support the use of table-driven tests: in easyb, for example, you might write a test like the following:

```
scenario "A Gold Card customer gets a discount based on the number of points
gained from previous sales", {
    given "Jill has a Gold Card with #numberOfPoints points"
    when "she buys an article"
    then "she should receive a #percentageDiscount discount"
    where "examples of percentage discounts for different point values", {
        numberOfPoints    =    [0,   50,   100,  200]
        percentageDiscount =   [0.0, 2.5,  5.0,  7.5]
    }
}
```

As you can see, table-driven tests are a powerful approach for specifying complex scenarios. High-level scenarios are only one part of our tests, but we still need to implement these scenarios and map them to steps where we concretely drive the GUI, which we'll discuss next.

Test Steps as Java or Groovy Classes

In all cases, Thucydides steps themselves are implemented in Java or Groovy classes as reusable methods. They may start their life as simple placeholders, marked as "pending" steps, as shown in Listing 10-3:

Listing 10-3. *Placeholders in use, marked as pending*

```
class BuyerSteps extends ScenarioSteps {
    BuyerSteps(Pages pages) {
        super(pages)
    }

    @Pending @Step
    def opens_home_page() {}

    @Pending @Step
    def chooses_category(name) {}

    @Pending @Step
    def chooses_by_keywords(name, keywords) {}
    ...
}
```

Java or Groovy classes can then be easily integrated into a continuous delivery system (e.g., based on Jenkins).

Turn Steps into Working Tests

Once this is done, the Thucydides reports will display the scenario steps for all to see, providing living documentation about how this feature is to be implemented (see Figure 10-3). This helps to document both what was requested and how it has been implemented. It is good practice to publish these reports automatically with each build and make them easily available to all team members (for example, by putting them on a project wiki). This helps product owners and testers ensure that everyone has the same understanding about exactly what needs to be implemented.

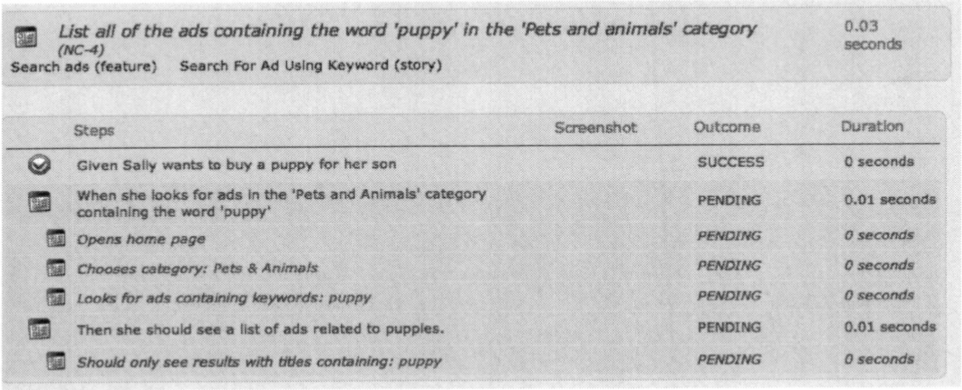

	List all of the ads containing the word 'puppy' in the 'Pets and animals' category (NC-4) Search ads (feature) Search For Ad Using Keyword (story)			0.03 seconds
	Steps	**Screenshot**	**Outcome**	**Duration**
✓	Given Sally wants to buy a puppy for her son		SUCCESS	0 seconds
	When she looks for ads in the 'Pets and Animals' category containing the word 'puppy'		PENDING	0.01 seconds
	Opens home page		PENDING	0 seconds
	Chooses category: Pets & Animals		PENDING	0 seconds
	Looks for ads containing keywords: puppy		PENDING	0 seconds
	Then she should see a list of ads related to puppies.		PENDING	0.01 seconds
	Should only see results with titles containing: puppy		PENDING	0 seconds

Figure 10-3. *Displaying the details of a pending test*

When the feature being developed becomes more stable, these steps can be fleshed out and turned into working tests. This essentially involves implementing the step methods so that they actually exercise the application under test.

Good step implementations tend to be relatively simple, and, for web testing, typically delegate to a Selenium 2 Page Object class (see below) to interact with the actual web page. When writing step implementations, developers should also keep in mind how to refactor existing steps when appropriate to make them more reusable across different tests.

An example of a simple set of steps implemented in Groovy is illustrated in Listing 10-4:

Listing 10-4. *Some Example Test Steps in Groovy*

```groovy
class BuyerSteps extends ScenarioSteps {
    BuyerSteps(Pages pages) {
        super(pages)
    }

    @Step
    def opens_home_page() {
        pages[HomePage].open()
    }

    @Step
    def chooses_category(name) {
        pages[HomePage].chooseCategory(name)
    }

    @Step
    def chooses_by_keywords(name, keywords) {
        pages[HomePage].searchByKeywords(keywords)
    }

    @Step
    def should_only_see_results_with_prices_bewteen(int minimumPrice,
                                                    int maximumPrice) {
        def prices = pages[SearchResultsPage].getPrices()
        prices.each {
            assert (it >= minimumPrice && it <= maximumPrice)
        }
    }
    ...
}
```

Tests are implemented by using the Page Object pattern, which we'll discuss next.

Page Object Pattern

These step methods make heavy use of the Page Object pattern. Page Object patterning is a tool and framework agnostic way of encapsulating the details about a web page inside a class, behind more business-focused method names. For example, in the step implementations listed above, we use terms such as chooseCategory and searchByKeyword, rather than referring to HTML fields or buttons. This not only makes the step implementations more readable, but it also makes maintenance easier, as changes to a particular page need only be made in the corresponding Page Object, rather than in every test that uses that page. In a nutshell, a Page Object models areas of your GUI that your tests interact with as objects within the test code. The pattern facilitates code reuse (by reducing duplicated code: if the UI changes, the fix need only be applied in one place) and maintenance (code logic and page are separated).[8]

Both Selenium 2 and Thucydides provide strong support for the Page Object pattern in order to make the actual implementation of web page interactions easier to write and maintain. An extract from a simple Page Object class using Thucydides is shown in Listing 10-5:

Listing 10-5. *A Simple Page Object Using Thucydides*

```
class ClassifiedAdsPage extends PageObject {
    WebElement search;
    ...
    NewsClassifiedPage(WebDriver driver) {
        super(driver)
    }
    def chooseCategory(name) {
    findBy('.name').then(By.partialLinkText(name)).then().click()
    }
    def searchByKeywords(keywords) {
        element(search).typeAndEnter(keywords)
    }
    ...
}
```

We'll now look at how to set up reporting for our tests.

Reporting on the Test Outcomes

As the project progresses, stories will be implemented and acceptance tests will pass. The relative number of passing acceptance tests gives a clear picture of how much has been achieved as well as an idea of how much work remains to be done (see Figure 10-4).

---

[8]For more information on Page Objects see
http://code.google.com/p/selenium/wiki/PageObjects.

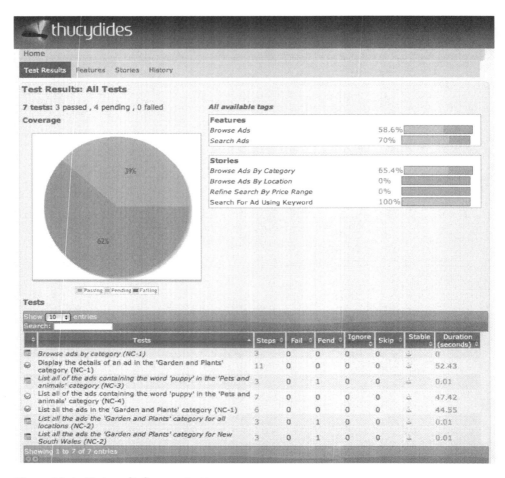

Figure 10-4. *Test results for a project in progress*

Knowing the number of steps involved in an automated example of an acceptance criteria is also useful. As a rule, the more steps involved in playing out an acceptance criteria, the more complex the corresponding feature is to implement. So it is beneficial to report not only the number of passing and pending tests, but also the relative complexity of the corresponding features, based on the number of steps involved in their tests. Indeed, this can give a more balanced measure of progress than just the number of passing tests.

It is also useful to be able to drill down into a particular feature to focus on the number of passing and pending tests for that feature. An important part of ATDD reporting is to be able to see both the overall picture but also to be able to zone in on a particular feature and to evaluate how ready it is in terms of the number and quality of the corresponding automated acceptance criteria.

Providing Living Documentation

ATDD techniques should also provide a form of living documentation, tracing the business goals and requested features all the way down to narrative, illustrated examples of how these features have been implemented. Living documentation not only helps express specifications in a way that all project members understand, but it also ensures that these specifications are always up to date; if for some reason the specification no longer matches the real behavior of the system, the corresponding test will fail. So these living specifications become a unique source of truth about what the system is intended to do, something that also becomes an invaluable resource when it comes to making changes to the system.

As illustrated in Figure 10-5, the reports for an implemented feature show both the high-level business goals (in the form of the given-when-then phrases) and the steps that illustrate how that goal is achieved.

	List all of the ads containing the word 'puppy' in the 'Pets and animals' category (NC-4)			46.03 seconds
	Search ads (feature) Search For Ad Using Keyword (story)			

	Steps	Screenshot	Outcome	Duration
✓	Given Sally wants to buy a puppy for her son		SUCCESS	0 seconds
✓	When she looks for ads in the 'Pets and Animals' category containing the word 'puppy'		SUCCESS	44.53 seconds
✓	Opens home page		SUCCESS	26.18 seconds
✓	Chooses category: Pets & Animals		SUCCESS	7.97 seconds
✓	Looks for ads containing keywords: puppy		SUCCESS	10 seconds
✓	Then she should see a list of ads related to puppies.		SUCCESS	1.49 seconds
✓	Should only see results with titles containing: puppy		SUCCESS	1.04 seconds

Figure 10-5. *Test reports also provide a form of living documentation*

Different stakeholders, particularly developers and product owners, can also flip through the corresponding screenshots to see how this implementation plays out against a running application. The screenshots are useful for debugging purposes when tests fail. This not only acts as part of the living documentation, but can also help the business owners build confidence in the quality of the automated tests.

Conclusion

DevOps is not feasible without both adequate suites of automated tests and a high degree of confidence in these tests. Specification by example provides a way to help build this confidence, first by expressing requirements in high-level business terms and then by automating these requirements in a way that provides a set of living documentation detailing both which requirements were requested and how they have been implemented. And, moving forward, this living documentation provided by the automated specifications provides both a single source of truth about the application's behavior and also a set of regression tests protecting it against unwanted change.

Moving On

This chapter closes the book. After learning about the fundamentals of DevOps, we continued our journey to the three different views on DevOps: metrics and measurement view, process view, and technical view.

DevOps helps to bridge the gap between development and operations and streamlines the overall software delivery process. With DevOps, improving the flow of features by reducing the batch size and cycle time is as important as improving delivery by automatic releasing and decoupling deployment and release. Quality is an inherent part of the development and delivery processes. Good cycle time is an example of a leading quality attribute that can help to bridge development and operations. But supporting quality attributes (e.g., test coverage or coffee supply) are also important. Patterns should be applied to improve quality, for example, by distinguishing between internal and external quality, using scenarios to describe quality, and emphasizing the test automation mix and inject quality gates.

Above all, applying the DevOps approach is a change of mindset. It is essential to build a team of Devs and Ops, which is aligned with shared incentives.

Fast feedback is not only gained through implementing a thorough degree of automation. Fast feedback is also a topic that is heavily related to the software development and delivery processes. There are different ways to implement and discuss DevOps and how to extend or embed the one party to the other. A holistic approach, using something like Kanban, can be a great choice to streamline the delivery process.

With DevOps, another area of interest that also relates to the process is setting up and maintaining good concepts. One example of a concept is nonfunctional requirements that are important for both development and operations. Conceptual deficits should be avoided and made visible early. They typically arise because of limited rationality, complex and dynamic environments, or moral hazard. Recipes to detect and minimize conceptual deficits include fostering traceability, checking nonfunctional requirements, and aligning goals.

Processes should be implemented by tools. Integrating the right tools is important for DevOps. Major parts of the releasing process should be automated. Important patterns here include using delivery pipelines, baselines, shared version numbers, automatic versioning, and release containers and by applying task-based development. A release consists of many different artifact types, including source code, build scripts, database elements, infrastructure as code, and acceptance tests.

We've covered all these different aspects. You should now be ready to get started with DevOps. So why wait? Let's go!

I hope that you've enjoyed reading the book as much as I've enjoyed writing it. I wish you all the best and much success with DevOps!

Index